LearningExpress Skill Builders Practice

501 Reading Comprehension Questions

 Published in the United States by LearningExpress, LLC, New York.

Library of Congress Cataloging-in-Publication Data

501 reading comprehension questions

p. cm.

ISBN 1–57685–201–6

1. Reading comprehension—Problems, exercises, etc. I. LearningExpress (Organization) II. Title: Five hundred one reading comprehension questions. III. Title: Five hundred and one reading comprehension questions.

LB1050.45.A15 1999

428.4'3'076—dc21 98–47904

CIP

Printed in the United States of America

9 8 7 6 5 4 3

First Edition

For Further Information

For information on LearningExpress, other LearningExpress products, or bulk sales, please call or write to us at:

LearningExpress™
900 Broadway
Suite 604
New York, NY 10003
212-995-2566

LearningExpress is an affiliated company of Random House, Inc.

Distributed to the retail trade by Random House, Inc., as agent for LearningExpress, LLC.

Visit LearningExpress on the World Wide Web at www.learnx.com.

ISBN 1–57685–201–6

SKILL BUILDERS PRACTICE TITLES ARE THE PERFECT COMPANIONS TO OUR SKILL BUILDERS BOOKS.

Reading Comprehension Success	ISBN 1–57685–126–5
Vocabulary and Spelling Success	ISBN 1–57685–127–3
Reasoning Skills Success	ISBN 1–57685–116–8
Writing Skills Success	ISBN 1–57685–128–1
Practical Math Success	ISBN 1–57685–129–X

What people are saying about LearningExpress *Skill Builders...*

"Works perfectly! ...an excellent program for preparing students for success on the new Regent's Exam. I love the format, as well as the tips on active reading and study skills. And the pre- and post-tests help me in assessing my class' reading abilities."

—Betty Hodge, 11th Grade English Teacher, Lancaster High School, NY

"The book provides help—help with understanding—for learners seeking to increase their vocabularies and improve their spelling."

—Rose C. Lobat, Jewish Community Center of Staten Island, NY

"I love this book! It is easy to use and extremely user-friendly, and the end results are outstanding."

—Janelle Mason

"If you are still dangling your participles, watching your sentences run on, and feeling irregular about verbs, check out this book. Recommended for the school, workplace, or even home for handy reference."

—Julie Pfeiffer, Middletown Public Library

"I used *Writing Skills Success* and *Practical Math Success* in my JTPA classes. They're excellent, concise tools and offered quick, precise ways to get the basics across."

— R. Eddington, JTPA Program Director

CONTENTS

Introduction 1

Questions 5

Answers 149

INTRODUCTION

Have trouble with reading comprehension questions on tests? Want to know how to improve your reading ability or your speed at reading with understanding? Want to have fun, testing your mettle with a whole lot of reading questions? This book is for you. Read on to find out why.

Maybe you like to read and just got this book to help you brush up your skills for an important test. If so, that's fine. In fact, you can skip this part of the Introduction—or the Introduction entirely—and go straight to the questions.

But maybe you're one of those millions of people who have trouble with reading, especially with reading carefully while reading quickly. If so, this introduction is meant for you.

First, know that you're not alone. It's a fact that some people relate more easily, say, to numbers or to working with their hands. And that's okay. Still, it's a fact of life that no other general skill is called on more regularly—in work, play, and just plain living—than reading. The good news is that reading well is a skill that can be developed with practice. This book will help, but something else will help even more. If you're serious about developing your reading comprehension skills, go to the library or a bookstore and pick out books on subjects that you find fascinating.

A young relative of mine, a talented athlete and musician, hated to read. There were three reasons: He'd never been read to as a child; he'd spent too much time during his young years in front of the TV; and he'd had bad experiences in grade school that caused his self-esteem to plummet. Then one day, at the beginning of junior high, he received the birthday gift that's universally detested by non-readers: a book. This one, though, was about skydiving. The book was, in fact, a little too old for him, but he was fascinated by the subject so he opened it. And loved it. Later, his mom caught him reading a bestseller about climbing Mt. Everest, and a little after that an actual classic, Jack London's tales of blizzards and wolves in the frozen North, *The Call of the Wild.*

Reading has never become Justin's first love—that's mountain-climbing and hiking in grizzly bear country, which scares most of the rest of us silly—but he does like to read now, does it by choice, and always carries a paperback along with his camping gear.

Nobody sat Justin down and forced him to *like* to read. It wouldn't have worked. And if you've always been a non-reader, you shouldn't force yourself, either. Reading isn't supposed to be grim—it's supposed to be fun, interesting, and enlightening. You can make it that way and still get the requisite practice that'll develop your skill. Wherever your true interests lie—whether it's doll-making or the Stock Market—that's where you should start.

An Overview

501 Reading Questions begins with short, easy, general interest passages that ask for the identification of explicit details and main ideas—that is, facts and ideas that are spelled out in the reading passage. Fairly simple job instructions follow this part, along with much more complex—but still explicit—passages on science and other difficult technical subjects. The book then moves on to more subtle, implicit material, to fiction, poetry, and related subjects—the kinds where you really have to put your thinking cap on to understand the reading and answer the questions.

The book is divided into sets that should take about 20 minutes to complete. Preceding each set is a hint on how to approach the particular task that faces the student.

Answers to each of the 501 questions are at the back of the book. Each answer is fully explained, so that if you have trouble with a particular question, you can see how you might have tackled that question or where you could have found the answer in the passage.

How to Use This Book

This book—which can be used alone, in combination with the LearningExpress publication, *Reading Comprehension Success in 20 Minutes a Day*, or along with another basic text of your choice—will give you practice in dealing with a range of types of reading, from general interest, to job instructions, to entertainment pieces, to fiction, poetry, and philosophy. Practice on the 501 reading questions in this book should help alleviate your reading anxiety, too!

WORKING ON YOUR OWN

If you are working alone to brush up on the basics and prepare for a test in connection with a job or school, you will probably want to use the book in combination with a basic text or with *Reading Comprehension Success in 20 Minutes a Day.* It will be helpful to read a summary of, say, how to approach explicit material or implicit material or poetry, and then proceed to practice. If you're fairly sure of your basic reading skills, however, you can use *501 Reading Questions* by itself.

Use the answer key at the end of the book not only to find out if you got the right answer but also to learn how to tackle the same kind of question next time. Every answer is explained. Make sure you understand the explanations—usually by going back to the passage—before going on to the next set.

Learn by doing. It's an old lesson, tried and true. And it's the tool this book is designed to give you.

TUTORING OTHERS

501 Reading Questions will work very well in combination with almost any basic reading or English text. You will probably find it most helpful to give the student a brief lesson in the particular kind of reading they'll be learning and then have them spend the remainder of the class or session reading the passages and answering the questions. Afterward, a brief review session will probably be helpful.

You will especially want to impress upon them the importance of learning by doing and of reading on their own, something they're fascinated by, for the pure joy of it.

ADDITIONAL RESOURCES

Following are the names of reading books you might want to buy or take out of the library if you prefer to study on your own. After that, there's a list of suggested books that will help you practice the skills you're learning.

- *Reading Comprehension Success in 20 Minutes a Day* by Elizabeth Chesla (LearningExpress)
- *Reading Smart* by Nicholas Reid Schaffzin (Princeton Review)
- *REA's Reading Comprehension Builder for Admission & Standardized Tests* (Research & Education Association)
- *10 Real SATs* (College Board)

SUGGESTED READING LIST

Reading *about* reading and answering reading test questions are all well and good, but the best way to improve your reading ability is to *read.* Here is a list of books, organized by subject categories. Choose a category that interests you, and try some of the books listed there.

Science Fiction

Fahrenheit 451 by Ray Bradbury
The Left Hand of Darkness by Ursula LeGuin
Stranger in a Strange Land by Robert Heinlein
1984 by George Orwell
Jurassic Park by Michael Crighton

Science/Medicine

The Lives of a Cell by Lewis Thomas
Mortal Lessons by Richard Selzer

Fantasy

The Hobbit by J. R. R. Tolkien
On a Pale Horse by Piers Anthony

Autobiography

The Autobiography of Malcolm X by Malcolm X
The Story of My Life by Helen Keller
The Diary of Anne Frank by Anne Frank
The Heroic Slave by Frederick Douglas
I Know Why the Caged Bird Sings by Maya Angelou
Having Our Say by Sarah L. and Elizabeth Delaney
Black Boy by Richard Wright
Everything I Need to Know I Learned in Kindergarten by Robert Fulghum

Historical/Social Issues

Of Mice and Men by John Steinbeck
The Color Purple by Alice Walker

The Last of the Mohicans
by James Fenimore Cooper
To Kill a Mockingbird by Harper Lee
The Joy Luck Club by Amy Tan
The Sun Also Rises by Ernest Hemingway
The Lord of the Flies by William Golding
Dangerous Minds by LouAnne Johnson
Schindler's List by Thomas Keneally

War

Red Badge of Courage by Stephen Crane
All Quiet on the Western Front
by Erich Maria Remarque
Hiroshima by John Hersey

Coming of Age

A Separate Peace by John Knowles
The Catcher in the Rye by J. D. Salinger
The House on Mango Street by Sandra Cisneros

Short Stories

The short stories of Ernest Hemingway
Love Life by Bobbie Ann Mason
Girls at War by Chinua Achebe
The Stories of Eva Luna by Isabel Allende

Inspirational/Spiritual

A Simple Path by Mother Theresa
The Tibetan Book of Living and Dying
by Sogyal Rinpoche
Care of the Soul by Thomas Moore
Hinds' Feet on High Places by Hannah Hurnard
The Tao of Pooh and *The Te of Piglet*
by Benjamin Hoff
The Holy Bible
The Koran
Tao Te Ching by Lao Tzu

Detective/Thriller

Agatha Christie's murder mysteries
A Time To Kill, The Client by John Grisham
The "A is for . . . " series by Sue Grafton
Novels by Sara Paretsky
Sherlock Holmes stories by
Sir Arthur Conan Doyle

Mythology

Mythology by Edith Hamilton
American Indian Myths and Legends by Richard Erdoes and Alfonso Ortiz

501 READING COMPREHENSION QUESTIONS

This book begins with simple, straightforward reading passages and ends with ones that are longer and much more complex. The passages are accompanied by questions that progress from asking you to identify explicit information to ones that ask you to make difficult inferences. The passages and questions are arranged in convenient short sets, each of which will probably take about 20 minutes to complete. However, don't worry too much about timing, and if you're going through the book with a group, don't compare your progress with anyone else's. Sets that may be easy for you may be difficult for others and vice-versa. A lot depends on your background and interests. Just relax and enjoy the mental exercise of reading.

SET 1 (Answers begin on page 149.)

Start off with these short, easy passages and questions. Most ask you to identify only explicit ideas and details, although a few may require that you make simple inferences. Like a good detective, begin by looking for the basic facts of the case.

Rehabilitation is a constructive way to reduce crime and generally improve the criminal justice system in a humane way. The system's current emphasis on punishment is a failure. Without rehabilitation before and after their discharge from prison, offenders will usually commit more crimes.

1. The paragraph best supports the statement that
   a. prisons should be replaced by humane rehabilitation centers
   b. without rehabilitation, criminals will invariably commit more crimes
   c. if criminals are rehabilitated the crime rate will go down
   d. most prisons today are too overcrowded for effective rehabilitation

A recent idea in law enforcement is community-oriented policing. This concept is used effectively in Japan. In every Japanese neighborhood there are Kobans, or guard shacks, where a local police officer sits. Tokyo has thousands of Kobans. This system has made the Japanese feel safe walking around their cities.

2. The paragraph best supports the statement that
   a. Kobans are an inexpensive and efficient way to keep cities safe
   b. in Japan, police officers do not patrol the streets but sit in Kobans instead
   c. Americans would do well to study Japanese law-enforcement methods
   d. community-oriented policing has made the residents of Tokyo feel secure

Anyone who lives in a large, modern city has heard the familiar sound of electronic security alarms. Although these mechanical alarms are fairly recent, the idea of a security system is not new. The oldest alarm system was probably a few strategically placed dogs who would discourage intruders with a loud warning cry.

3. The paragraph best supports the statement that
   a. dogs are more reliable than electronic alarms
   b. city dwellers would be wise to use dogs for security
   c. mechanical alarm systems break down but dogs do not
   d. a dog is an older alarm device than is a mechanical alarm

The Fourth Amendment to the Constitution protects citizens against unreasonable searches and seizures. No search of a person's home or personal effects may be conducted without a written search warrant issued on probable cause. This means that a neutral judge must approve the factual basis justifying a search before it can be conducted.

4. The paragraph best supports the statement that the police cannot search a person's home or private papers unless they
   a. have obtained legal written authorization
   b. have irrefutable evidence of a crime
   c. first read the person his or her constitutional rights
   d. have requested that a judge be present

During colonial times in America, juries were encouraged to ask questions of the parties in the courtroom. The jurors were, in fact, expected to investigate the facts of the case themselves. If jurors conducted an investigation today, we would throw out the case.

5. The paragraph best supports the statement that

a. juries are less important today than they were in colonial times

b. courtrooms today are more efficient than they were in colonial times

c. jurors in colonial times were more informed than jurors today

d. the jury system in America has changed since colonial times

In cities throughout the country, there is a new direction in local campaign coverage. Frequently in local elections, journalists are not giving voters enough information to understand the issues and evaluate the candidates. The local news media devotes too much time to scandal and not enough time to policy.

6. This paragraph best supports the statement that the local news media

a. is not doing an adequate job when it comes to covering local campaigns

b. does not understand either campaign issues or politics

c. should learn how to cover politics by watching the national news media

d. has no interest in covering stories about local political events

The use of desktop computer equipment and software to create high-quality printing such as newsletters, business cards, letterhead, and brochures is called Desktop Publishing, or DTP. The most important part of any DTP project is planning. Before you begin, you should know your intended audience, the message you want to communicate, and what form your message will take.

7. The paragraph best supports the statement that

a. DTP is one way to become acquainted with a new business audience

b. computer software is continually being refined to produce more high-quality printing

c. the first stage of any proposed DTP project should be organization and design

d. the planning stage of any DTP project should include talking with the intended audience

Many office professionals today have an interest in replacing the currently used keyboard, known as the QWERTY keyboard, with a keyboard that can keep up with technological changes and make offices more efficient. The best choice is the Dvorak keyboard. Studies have shown that people using the Dvorak keyboard can type 20 to 30 percent faster and cut their error rate in half. Dvorak puts vowels and other frequently used letters right under the fingers(on the home row) where typists make 70 percent of their keystrokes.

8. The paragraph best supports the statement that the Dvorak keyboard

a. is more efficient than the QWERTY

b. has more keys right under the typists' fingers than the QWERTY

c. is favored by more typists than the QWERTY

d. is, on average, 70 percent faster than the QWERTY

Every year Americans use over one billion sharp objects to administer health care in their homes. These sharp objects include lancets, needles, and syringes. If not disposed of in puncture-resistant containers, they can injure sanitation workers. Sharp objects should be disposed of in hard plastic or metal containers with secure lids. The containers should be clearly marked and be puncture resistant.

9. The paragraph best supports the idea that sanitation workers can be injured if they

a. do not place sharp objects in puncture-resistant containers
b. come in contact with sharp objects that have not been placed in secure containers
c. are careless with sharp objects such as lancets, needles, and syringes in their homes
d. do not mark the containers they pick up with a warning that those containers contain sharp objects

There are no effective boundaries when it comes to pollutants. Studies have shown that toxic insecticides that have been banned in many countries are riding the wind from countries where they remain legal. Compounds such as DDT and toxaphene have been found in remote places like the Yukon and other Arctic regions.

10. The paragraph best supports the statement that

a. toxic insecticides such as DDT have not been banned throughout the world
b. many countries have ignored their own anti-pollution laws
c. DDT and toxaphene are the two most toxic insecticides in the world
d. even a worldwide ban on toxic insecticides would not stop the spread of DDT pollution

SET 2 (Answers begin on page 150.)

Remember, you don't have to have outside knowledge of the subject of the passage—the answers are always right there in the passage. This is the case with almost all reading comprehension tests you may take.

The criminal justice system needs to change. The system could be more just if it allowed victims the opportunity to confront the person who has harmed them. Also, mediation between victims and their offenders would give the offenders a chance to apologize for the harm they have done.

11. This paragraph best supports the statement that victims of a crime should
a. learn to forgive their offenders
b. learn the art of mediation
c. insist that their offenders be punished
d. have the right to confront their offenders

One of the missions of the Peace Corps is to help the people of interested countries meet their need for trained men and women. People who work for the Peace Corps do so because they want to. But to keep the Peace Corps dynamic with fresh ideas, no staff member can work for the agency for more than five years.

12. The paragraph best supports the statement that Peace Corps employees
a. are highly intelligent people
b. must train for about five years
c. are hired for a limited term of employment
d. have both academic and work experience

More and more office workers telecommute from offices in their own homes. The upside of telecommuting is both greater productivity and greater flexibility. Telecommuters produce, on average, 20% more than if they were to work in an office, and their flexible schedule allows them to balance both their family and work responsibilities.

13. The paragraph best supports the statement that telecommuters
a. get more work done in a given time period than workers who travel to the office
b. produce a better quality work product than workers who travel to the office
c. are more flexible in their ideas than workers who travel to the office
d. would do 20% more work if they were to work in an office

Close-up images of Mars by the *Mariner 9* probe indicated networks of valleys that looked like the stream beds on Earth. These images also implied that Mars once had an atmosphere that was thick enough to trap the sun's heat. If this is true, something must have happened to Mars billions of years ago that stripped away the planet's atmosphere.

14. The paragraph best supports the statement that
a. Mars once had a thicker atmosphere than earth does
b. the *Mariner 9* probe took the first pictures of Mars
c. Mars now has little or no atmosphere
d. Mars is closer to the sun than Earth is

It is a myth that labor shortages today center mostly on computer jobs. Although it is true that the lack of computer-related skills accounts for many of the problems in today's job market, there is a lack of skilled labor in many different fields. There is a shortfall of uniformed police officers in many cities, for example, and a shortage of trained criminal investigators in some rural areas. These jobs may utilize computer skills, but are not essentially computer jobs.

15. The paragraph best supports the statement that

a. people with computer skills are in demand in police and criminal investigator jobs
b. unemployment in computer-related fields is not as widespread as some people think
c. there is a shortage of skilled workers in a variety of fields, including police work
d. trained criminal investigators are often underpaid in rural areas

After a snow or ice fall, the City streets are treated with ordinary rock salt. In some areas, the salt is combined with calcium chloride, which is more effective in below-zero temperatures and which melts ice better. This combination of salt and calcium chloride is also less damaging to foliage along the roadways.

16. In deciding whether to use ordinary rock salt or the salt and calcium chloride mxture on a particular street, which of the following is NOT a consideration?

a. the temperature at the time of treatment
b. the plants and trees along the street
c. whether there is ice on the street
d. whether the street is a main or secondary road

17. According to the above snow treatment directions, which of the following is true?

a. If the temperature is below zero, salt and calcium chloride is effective in treating snow- and ice-covered streets.
b. Crews must wait until the snow or ice stops falling before salting streets.
c. The City always salts major roads first.
d. If the snowfall is light, the City will not salt the streets as this would be a waste of the salt supply.

The City has distributed standardized recycling containers to all households with directions that read: "We would prefer that you use this new container as your primary recycling container as this will expedite pick-up of recyclables. Additional recycling containers may be purchased from the City."

18. According to the directions, each household

a. may only use one recycling container
b. must use the new recycling container
c. should use the new recycling container
d. must buy a new recycling container

19. According to the directions, which of the following is true about the new containers?

a. The new containers are far better than other containers in every way.
b. The new containers will help increase the efficiency of the recycling program.
c. The new containers hold more than the old containers did.
d. The new containers are less expensive than the old.

Ratatouille is a dish that has grown in popularity worldwide over the last few years. It features eggplant, zucchini, tomato, peppers, and garlic, chopped, mixed together, sautéed briefly, and finally, cooked slowly over low heat. As the vegetables cook slowly, they make their own broth, which may be extended with a little tomato paste. The name *ratatouille* comes from the French word *touiller*, meaning to stir or mix together.

20. Which of the following show the correct order of steps for making ratatouille?

a. chop vegetables, add tomato paste, stir or mix together
b. mix the vegetables together, sauté them, and add tomato paste
c. cook the vegetables slowly, mix them together, add tomato paste
d. add tomato paste to extend the broth and cook slowly over low heat

21. Ratatouille can best be described as a

a. French pastry
b. sauce to put over vegetables
c. pasta dish extended with tomato paste
d. vegetable stew

SET 3 (Answers begin on page 150.)

Here are more brief, fairly simple passages. To avoid making errors, be sure to read closely and carefully, as some answers that seem obvious may be wrong.

Law enforcement officers often do not like taking time from their regular duties to testify in court, but testimony is an important part of an officer's job. To be good witnesses, officers should keep complete notes detailing any potentially criminal or actionable incidents. When on the witness stand, officers may refer to those notes to refresh their memories about particular events. It is also very important for officers to listen carefully to the questions asked by the lawyers and to provide only the information requested. Officers should never volunteer opinions or any extra information that is beyond the scope of a question.

22. According to the passage, an officer who is testifying in court

a. may be questioned by both the judge and the lawyers

b. should volunteer his or her time as an important civic duty

c. may appreciate taking a break from routine assignments

d. may refer to his or her notes while on the witness stand

23. The paragraph best supports the statement that a poor police witness might

a. rely on memory alone when testifying in court

b. hold an opinion about the guilt or innocence of a suspect before the trial is over

c. rely too much on notes and not enough on experience at the crime scene

d. be unduly influenced by prosecution lawyers when giving testimony

24. According to the passage, testifying in court is

a. a significant part of a law enforcement officer's job

b. difficult, because lawyers try to get witnesses to volunteer information

c. less stressful for police officers than for other witnesses

d. often futile, because criminals frequently get off on technicalities

The Competitive Civil Service system is designed to give applicants fair and equal treatment and to ensure that federal applicants are hired based on objective criteria. Hiring has to be based solely on candidates' knowledge, skills, and abilities (which you'll sometimes see abbreviated as *ksa*) and not on any external factors such as race, religion, sex, and so on. Whereas employers in the private sector can hire employees for subjective reasons, federal employers must be able to justify their decisions with objective evidence that the candidate is qualified.

25. The paragraph best supports the statement that

a. hiring in the private sector is inherently unfair

b. *ksa* are not as important as test scores to federal employers

c. federal hiring practices are simpler than those employed by the private sector

d. the civil service strives to hire on the basis of a candidate's abilities

26. The federal government's practice of hiring on the basis of *ksa* frequently results in the hiring of employees

a. based on race, religion, sex, and so forth

b. who are unqualified for the job

c. who are qualified for the job

d. on the basis of subjective judgment

It is well-known that the world urgently needs adequate distribution of food, so that everyone gets enough. Adequate distribution of medicine is just as urgent. Medical expertise and medical supplies need to be redistributed throughout the world so that people in emerging nations will have proper medical care.

27. This paragraph best supports the statement that
- a. the majority of the people in the world have no medical care
- b. medical resources in emerging nations have diminished in the past few years
- c. not enough doctors give time and money to those in need of medical care
- d. many people who live in emerging nations are not receiving proper medical care

In the past, suggesting a gas tax has usually been thought of as political poison. But that doesn't seem to be the case today. Several states are pushing bills in their state legislatures that would cut income or property taxes and make up the revenue with taxes on fossil fuel.

28. The paragraph best supports the statement that
- a. gas taxes produce more revenue than income taxes
- b. states with low income tax rates are increasing their gas taxes
- c. state legislators no longer fear increasing gas taxes
- d. taxes on fossil fuels are more popular than property taxes

One of the warmest winters on record has put consumers in the mood to spend money. Spending is likely to be the strongest in thirteen years. During the month of February, sales of existing single-family homes hit an annual record rate of 4.75 million.

29. The paragraph best supports the statement that
- a. more people buy houses in the month of February than in any other month
- b. during the winter months, the prices of single-family homes are the lowest
- c. there were about 4 million homes for sale during the month of February
- d. warm winter weather is likely to affect the rate of home sales

SET 4 (Answers begin on page 151.)

Try your hand at identifying the *explicit* (or *stated*) *main idea* of each of these brief passages. Remember that there is a difference between the subject of a passage and its main idea. When looking for the main idea, look for one that best encompasses or sums up the passage as a whole.

Recent history has been about ideologies: communism versus capitalism, fascism versus democracy. But the end of the cold war has resulted in many subtle challenges throughout the world. Today, global politics is being reconfigured along cultural lines. Political boundaries are increasingly redrawn along ethnic and religious lines.

30. The main idea of the passage is that, since the cold war,

a. in most countries religion and ethnicity have become more important than communism or capitalism
b. in countries throughout the world, religion and ethnicity have become more important than political ideology
c. in countries throughout the world, political boundaries should be redrawn
d. in most countries, fascism and communism no longer exist

Lawyer-bashing is on the increase in the United States. Lawyers are accused of lacking principles, clogging the justice system, and increasing the cost of liability insurance. Lawyers have received undeserved criticism. A lawyer is more likely than not to try to dissuade a client from litigation by offering to arbitrate and settle conflict.

31. The main idea of the paragraph is best expressed in which of the following statements from the passage?

a. Lawyer-bashing is on the increase in the United States.
b. Lawyers have received undeserved criticism.
c. Lawyers are accused of lacking principles.
d. A lawyer is more likely than not to try to dissuade a client from litigation by offering to arbitrate and settle conflict.

Whether or not you can accomplish a specific goal or meet a specific deadline depends first on how much time you need to get the job done. What should you do when the demands of the job exceed the time you have available? The best approach is to divide the project into smaller pieces. Different goals will have to be divided in different ways, but one seemingly unrealistic goal can often be accomplished by working on several smaller, more reasonable goals.

32. The main idea of the passage is that

a. jobs often remain only partially completed because of lack of time
b. the best way to complete projects is to make sure your goals are achievable
c. the best way to tackle a large project is to separate it into smaller parts
d. the best approach to a demanding job is to delegate responsibility

Due to downsizing and new technologies, the role of the traditional secretary is declining. At the same time, secretaries and administrative assistants are becoming much more important to businesses of all sizes. Although traditional jobs such as typist, stenographer, and data entry specialist have declined by about 33 percent, there has been a sharp increase in jobs such as clerical supervisor and medical and legal secretary.

33. The main idea of the paragraph is that
a. secretaries are less important now than they once were
b. many traditional secretaries have been promoted to clerical supervisors
c. due to downsizing, about 33 percent of all typists have recently become unemployed
d. advances in technology have contributed to the changing role of the secretary

For most judges, sentencing a person who has been convicted of a crime is a difficult decision. In the majority of jurisdictions throughout the country, judges have few sentencing options from which to choose. Generally, their options are confined to a fine, probation, or incarceration. Crimes, however, cover a wide spectrum of criminal behavior and motivation, and a wide variety of sanctions should be available.

34. The main idea of the paragraph is that
a. there should be laws that dictate which sentence a judge should hand down
b. someone other than a judge should be allowed to sentence a criminal
c. judges should be given more sentencing options from which to choose
d. more money should be spent on the criminal justice system

Before you begin to compose a business letter, sit down and think about your purpose in writing the letter. Do you want to request information, order a product, register a complaint, or apply for something? Do some brainstorming and gather information before you begin writing. Always keep your objective in mind.

35. The main idea of the passage is that
a. planning is an important part of writing a business letter
b. business letters are frequently complaint letters
c. brainstorming and writing take approximately equal amounts of time
d. many people neglect to plan ahead when they are writing a business letter

Keeping busy at important tasks is much more motivating than having too little to do. Today's employees are not afraid of responsibility. Most people are willing to take on extra responsibility in order to have more variety on their jobs. In addition, along with more responsibility should come the authority to carry out some important tasks independently.

36. The main idea of the paragraph is that
a. variety and independence on the job increase employee motivation
b. to avoid boredom, many people do more work than their jobs require of them
c. today's employees are demanding more independence than ever before
d. office jobs in the past have carried less responsibility than in the past

Managing job and family is not simple. Both commitments make strong demands on people and are sometimes in direct opposition to each other. Saying yes to one means saying no to the other, and stress can often result. Being realistic and creating a balance in life can help set priorities.

37. The main idea of the paragraph is that
a. most family responsibilities cause stress at home and at work
b. because it pays the bills, a job must take priority over other commitments
c. it is important to have a balance between job and family responsibilities
d. because they are so important, family duties must take priority over the job

Generation Xers are those people born roughly between 1965 and 1981. As employees, Generation Xers tend to be more challenged when they can carry out tasks independently. This makes Generation Xers the most entrepreneurial generation in history.

38. This paragraph best supports the statement that Generation Xers
a. work harder than people from other generations
b. have a tendency to be self-directed workers
c. tend to work in jobs that require risk-taking behavior
d. like to challenge their bosses' work attitudes

Answer questions 39 and 40 on the basis of the following passage.

Electronic mail (E-mail) has been in widespread use for more than a decade. E-mail simplifies the flow of ideas, connects people from distant offices, eliminates the need for meetings, and often boosts productivity. But E-mail should be carefully managed to avoid unclear and inappropriate communication. E-mail messages should be concise and limited to one topic. When complex issues need to be addressed, phone calls are still best.

39. The main idea of the paragraph is that E-mail
a. is not always the easiest way to connect people from distant offices
b. has changed considerably since it first began a decade ago
c. causes people to be unproductive when it is used incorrectly
d. is effective for certain kinds of messages but only if managed wisely

40. Which of the following would be the most appropriate title for the passage?
a. Appropriate Use of E-Mail
b. E-Mail's Popularity
c. E-Mail: The Ideal Form of Communication
d. Why Phone Calls Are Better than E-Mail

SET 5 (Answers begin on page 151.)

Here are more brief passages, each with a single primary focus. The main idea of each will be one that is somewhat general, rather than too narrow or detailed.

Children start out in a world where fantasy and imagination are not substantially different from experience. But as they get older, they are shocked to discover that the world in which people reliably exist is the physical world. Computer games and virtual reality are two ways in which children can come to terms with this dilemma.

41. The main idea of the paragraph is that computer games and virtual reality

a. can be important tools in children's lives
b. keep children from experiencing reality
c. help children to uncover shocking truths about the world
d. should take the place of children's fantasy worlds

Native American art often incorporates a language of abstract visual symbols. The artist gives a poetic message to the viewer, communicating the beauty of an idea, either by using religious symbols or a design from nature such as rain on leaves or sunshine on water. The idea communicated may even be purely whimsical, in which case the artist might start out with symbols developed from a bird's tracks or a child's toy.

42. The main idea of the passage is that Native American art

a. is purely poetic and dream-like
b. is usually abstract, although it can also be poetic and beautiful
c. communicates the beauty of ideas through the use of symbols
d. is sometimes purely whimsical

In criminal cases, the availability of readable fingerprints is often critical in establishing evidence of a major crime. It is necessary, therefore, to follow proper procedures when taking fingerprints. For elimination purposes, major case prints should be obtained from all persons who may have touched areas associated with a crime scene.

43. The main idea of the paragraph is that

a. Because fingerprints are so important in many cases, it is important to follow the correct course in taking them.
b. All fingerprints found at a crime scene should be taken and thoroughly investigated.
c. If the incorrect procedure is followed in gathering fingerprints, the ones taken may be useless.
d. The first step in investigating fingerprints is to eliminate those of non-suspects.

44. The paragraph best supports the statement that

a. no crimes can be solved without readable fingerprints
b. all persons who have touched an area in a crime scene are suspects
c. all fingerprints found at a crime scene are used in court as evidence
d. all persons who have touched a crime-scene area should be fingerprinted

Detectives who routinely investigate violent crimes can't help but become somewhat jaded. Paradoxically, the victims and witnesses with whom they work closely are often in a highly vulnerable and emotional state. The emotional fallout from a sexual assault, for example, can be complex and long lasting. Detectives must be trained to handle people in emotional distress and must be sensitive to the fact that for the victim the crime is not routine. At the same time, detectives must recognize the limits of their role and resist the temptation to act as therapists or social workers, instead referring victims to the proper agencies.

45. What is the main idea of the passage?

a. The best detectives do not become emotionally hardened by their jobs.
b. Victims of violent crime should be referred to therapists and social workers.
c. Detectives should be sensitive to the emotional state of victims of violent crime.
d. Detectives should be particularly careful in dealing with victims of sexual assault.

46. According to the passage, what is "paradoxical" about the detective's relationship to the victim?

a. Detectives know less about the experience of violent crime than do victims.
b. What for the detective is routine is a unique and profound experience for the victim.
c. Detectives must be sensitive to victims' needs but can't be social workers or psychologists.
d. Not only must detectives solve crimes, but they must also handle the victims with care.

47. Which of the following is NOT advocated by the passage for detectives who investigate violent crimes?

a. They should refer victims to appropriate support services.
b. They should be aware of the psychological consequences of being victimized.
c. They should not become jaded.
d. They should not become too personally involved with victims' problems.

Although romanticized in fiction, the job of a private investigator is often actually boring. The real PI can spend hours or days looking into a not-particularly-lucrative insurance fraud scheme or sitting outside a sleazy motel waiting to catch some not-particularly-attractive philandering husband or wife of a client in the act. In fact, there would be very few private investigators in detective fiction if their jobs had to be portrayed realistically.

48. Which of the following is the main idea of the passage?

a. Private investigators do not make much money and their jobs are often sleazy and boring.
b. The romanticized life of the fictional private investigator is nothing like the sordid, dull reality.
c. If they had it to do over again, most PIs would not choose the career of private investigation.
d. Private investigation often concerns adultery, insurance fraud, and other petty matters.

49. The paragraph best supports the statement that private investigators

a. routinely do work related to industrial or family disputes
b. usually have disreputable clients
c. embellish their experience so they can write more exciting detective fiction
d. sometimes choose their line of work because they think it will be romantic

SET 6 (Answers begin on page 152.)

The passages will begin to be somewhat longer now. Remember to base your answers on information that is clearly stated or implied in the passage, rather than depending on any special knowledge you may have of the subject.

On occasion, corrections officers may be involved in receiving a confession from an inmate under their care. Sometimes, one inmate may confess to another inmate, who may be motivated to pass the information on to corrections officers. Often, however, these confessions are obtained by placing an undercover agent, posing as an inmate, in a cell with the prisoner. On the surface, this may appear to violate the principles of the constitutional Fifth Amendment privilege against self-incrimination. However, the courts have found that the Fifth Amendment is intended to protect suspects from coercive interrogation, which is present when a person is in custody and is subject to official questioning. In the case of an undercover officer posing as an inmate, the questioning does not appear to be official; therefore, confessions obtained in this manner are not considered coercive.

50. According to the passage, corrections officers
a. are allowed to question imprisoned inmates about their crimes
b. sometimes go undercover and receive confessions from inmates
c. should try to become friendly with inmates in order to gather information
d. should always read inmates their rights before talking to them

51. According to the passage, prison inmates
a. sometimes make confessions to fellow inmates
b. lose their privilege against self-incrimination
c. do not know they can refuse to answer corrections officers' questions
d. may be coerced into confessing

52. The privilege against self-incrimination can be found in
a. a Supreme Court opinion
b. prison rules and regulations
c. state law governing prisons
d. the U.S. Constitution

An ecosystem is a group of animals and plants living in a specific region and interacting with one another and with their physical environment. Ecosystems include physical and chemical components, such as soils, water, and nutrients, that support the organisms living there. These organisms may range from large animals to microscopic bacteria. Ecosystems also can be thought of as the interactions among all organisms in a given habitat; for instance, one species may serve as food for another. People are part of the ecosystems where they live and work. Human activities can harm or destroy local ecosystems unless actions such as land development for housing or businesses are carefully planned to conserve and sustain the ecology of the area. An important part of ecosystem management involves finding ways to protect and enhance economic and social well-being while protecting local ecosystems.

53. What is the main idea of the passage?

a. An ecosystem is a community that includes animals, plants, and microscopic bacteria.
b. Human activities can do great damage to local ecosystems, so human communities should be cautiously planned.
c. In managing the ecology of an area, it is important to protect both human interests and the interests of other members of local ecosystems.
d. People should remember that they are a part of the ecosystems where they live and work.

54. Which of the following best sums up activities within an ecosystem?

a. predator-prey relationships
b. interactions among all members
c. human-animal interactions
d. human relationship with the environment

55. An ecosystem can most accurately be defined as a

a. geographical area
b. community
c. habitat
d. protected environment

SET 7 (Answers begin on page 152.)

In most tests of reading comprehension and unless directed otherwise, you should assume that the information in the passages is correct, even if you disagree with it.

One of the most hazardous conditions a firefighter will ever encounter is a backdraft (also known as a smoke explosion). A backdraft can occur in the hot-smoldering phase of a fire when burning is incomplete and there is not enough oxygen to sustain the fire. Unburned carbon particles and other flammable products, combined with the intense heat, may cause instantaneous combustion if more oxygen reaches the fire.

Firefighters should be aware of the conditions that indicate the possibility for a backdraft to occur. When there is a lack of oxygen during a fire, the smoke becomes filled with carbon dioxide or carbon monoxide and turns dense gray or black. Other warning signs of a potential backdraft are little or no visible flame, excessive heat, smoke leaving the building in puffs, muffled sounds, and smoke-stained windows.

Proper ventilation will make a backdraft less likely. Opening a room or building at the highest point allows heated gases and smoke to be released gradually. However, suddenly breaking a window or opening a door is a mistake, as it allows oxygen to rush in, causing an explosion.

56. A backdraft is a dangerous condition for firefighters mainly because
a. there is not enough oxygen for breathing
b. the heat is extremely intense
c. the smoke is dangerously thick
d. an explosion occurs

57. Which of the following is NOT mentioned as a potential backdraft warning sign?
a. windows stained with smoke
b. flames shooting up from the building
c. puffs of smoke leaving the building
d. more intense heat than usual

58. To prevent the possibility of a backdraft, a firefighter should
a. carry an oxygen tank
b. open a door to allow gases to escape
c. make an opening at the top of the building
d. break a window to release carbon particles

59. When compared with a hot, smoldering fire, a fire with visible, high-reaching flames
a. has more oxygen available for combustion
b. has more carbon dioxide available for consumption
c. produces more dense gray smoke
d. is more likely to cause a backdraft

In the 1966 Supreme Court decision *Miranda v. Arizona*, the court held that before the police can obtain statements from a person arrested and subjected to an interrogation, the person must be given a *Miranda* warning. This warning means that a person must be told that he or she has the right to remain silent during the police interrogation and the right to have an attorney present during questioning. Violation of these rights means that any statement that the person makes is not admissible in a court hearing.

Police officers must read suspects their Miranda rights upon taking them into custody. When a suspect who is merely being questioned incriminates himself, he might later claim to have been in custody, and seek to have the case dismissed on the grounds of having been unapprised of his Miranda rights. In such cases, a judge must make a determination as to whether or not a reasonable person would have believed himself to be in custody, based on certain criteria. The judge must determine whether the suspect was questioned in a threatening manner (for example, it might be considered threatening if the suspect were seated while both officers remained standing) and whether the suspect was aware that he or she was free to leave at any time. Officers must be aware of these criteria and take care not to give suspects grounds for later claiming they believed themselves to be in custody.

60. What is the main idea of the passage?
a. Officers must remember to read all suspects their Miranda rights.
b. Judges, not police officers, make the final determination as to whether or not a suspect was in custody.
c. Officers who are merely questioning a suspect must not give the suspect the impression that he or she is in custody.
d. Miranda rights need not be read to all suspects before questioning.

TOO NARROW!

61. According to the passage, when is a suspect not in custody?
a. when free to refuse to answer questions
b. when free to leave the police station
c. when apprised of his or her Miranda rights
d. when free to obtain and consult a lawyer

62. When must police officers read Miranda rights to a suspect?
a. while questioning the suspect
b. before taking the suspect to the police station
c. while placing the suspect under arrest
d. before releasing the suspect

63. The passage indicates that a police officer who is questioning a suspect who is NOT under arrest must inform the suspect of his or her
a. Miranda rights
b. freedom to leave
c. right to an attorney
d. right to make a phone call

SET 8 (Answers begin on page 152.)

Remember that to be a skillful reader, you must be an active reader. If this is your book, try marking up the text, underlining important points and making notes in the margins. If the book isn't yours, make notes to yourself on a separate sheet of paper.

When the current measure used to calculate poverty levels was introduced in 1963, the poverty line for a family of two adults and two children was about $3,100. In 1992, there were 36.9 million people, or 14.5 percent of the U.S. population, with incomes below the poverty line. A proposed new way of measuring poverty levels would include for the first time the effects of work-related expenses such as transportation costs and child care costs on families' available income.

The largest effect of the new measure would be a decrease in the percentage of people in families receiving cash welfare who fall under the poverty line, and an increase in the percentage of people in working families who fall under it. People in families receiving cash welfare would make up 30 percent of the poor under the new measure, compared with 40 percent under the current measure. In contrast, people in working families would make up 59 percent of the poor under the new measure, compared with 51 percent under the current measure.

64. According to the 1963 standards, the current number of poor working families is approximately what proportion of the population?

a. 30 percent
b. 40 percent
c. 51 percent
d. 60 percent

65. One difference between the current and proposed measures is the fact that

a. the proposed measure identifies fewer working poor
b. the current measure identifies fewer working poor
c. the proposed measure disregards expenses for basic needs
d. the current measure includes more people with health insurance

Firefighters know that the dangers of motor-vehicle fires are too often overlooked. In the United States, 1 out of 5 fires involves motor vehicles, resulting each year in 600 deaths, 2,600 civilian injuries, and 1,200 injuries to firefighters. The reason for so many injuries and fatalities is that a vehicle can generate heat of up to 1500°F. (The boiling point of water is 212°F., and the cooking temperature for most foods is 500°F.)

Because of the intense heat generated in a vehicle fire, parts of the car or truck may burst, causing debris to shoot great distances and turning bumpers, tire rims, drive shafts, axles, and even engine parts into lethal shrapnel. Gas tanks may rupture and spray highly flammable fuel. In addition, hazardous materials such as battery acid, even without burning, can cause serious injury.

Vehicle fires can also produce toxic gases. Carbon monoxide, which is produced during a fire, is an odorless and colorless gas but in high concentrations is deadly. Firefighters must wear self-contained breathing devices and full protective fire-resistant gear when attempting to extinguish a vehicle fire.

66. One reason that firefighters wear self-contained breathing devices is to protect themselves against
a. debris
b. intense heat
c. flammable fuels
d. carbon monoxide

67. The passage suggests that most injuries in motor-vehicle fires are caused by
a. battery acid
b. odorless gases
c. extremely high temperatures
d. firefighters' mistakes

68. The main focus of this passage is
a. how firefighters protect themselves
b. the dangers of motor-vehicle fires
c. the amount of heat generated in some fires
d. the dangers of odorless gases

69. The cooking temperature for food (500°F) is most likely included in the passage to show the reader
a. how hot motor-vehicle fires really are
b. at what point a motor-vehicle will explode
c. why motor-vehicle fires produce toxic gases
d. why 1 out of 5 fires involves a motor vehicle

70. One reason that firefighters must be aware of the possibility of carbon monoxide in motor-vehicle fires is because carbon monoxide
a. is highly concentrated
b. cannot be seen or smelled
c. cannot be protected against
d. can shoot great distances into the air

SET 9 (Answers begin on page 153.)

Again, try marking up the passages or taking notes. As newspaper reporters do, ask the questions, "Who? What? When? Where? How? and Why?"

On February 3, 1956, Autherine Lucy became the first African-American student to attend the University of Alabama, although the dean of women refused to allow Autherine to live in a university dormitory. White students rioted in protest of her admission, and the federal government had to assume command of the Alabama National Guard in order to protect her. Nonetheless, on her first day in class, Autherine bravely took a seat in the front row. She remembers being surprised that the professor of the class appeared not to notice she was even in class. Later she would appreciate his seeming indifference, as he was one of only a few professors to speak out in favor of her right to attend the university.

For protection, Autherine was taken in and out of classroom buildings by the back door and driven from class to class by an assistant to the president of the university. The students continued to riot, and one day the windshield of the car she was in was broken. University officials suspended her, saying it was for her own safety. When her attorney issued a statement in her name protesting her suspension, the university used it as grounds for expelling her for insubordination. Although she never finished her education at the University of Alabama, Autherine Lucy's courage was an inspiration to African-American students who followed in her footsteps and desegregated universities all over the United States.

71. According to the passage, what did Autherine Lucy do on her first day at the University of Alabama?
a. She moved into a dormitory.
b. She sat in the front row of her class.
c. She became terrified of the white rioters.
d. She was befriended by the assistant to the president of the university.

72. Based on the information in the passage, which of the following best describes Autherine Lucy?
a. quiet and shy
b. courageous and determined
c. clever and amusing
d. overly-dramatic

73. When she began classes at the university, Autherine Lucy expected to
a. stand out from the other students
b. have the support of the university faculty
c. join an African-American organization for protection
d. be ridiculed by the professors

74. Autherine Lucy never graduated from the University of Alabama because she
a. moved to another state
b. transferred to another university
c. dropped out because of pressure from other students
d. was expelled for insubordination

75. According to the passage, which of the following is true?

a. The Alabama National Guard is normally under the command of the U.S. Army.
b. In 1956, the only segregated university in the United States was in Alabama.
c. Autherine Lucy was escorted to and from class by the university president's assistant.
d. A few white students at the university were pleased that Autherine Lucy was a student there.

The human body can tolerate only a small range of temperature, especially when the person is engaged in vigorous activity. Heat reactions usually occur when large amounts of water and/or salt are lost through excessive sweating following strenuous exercise. When the body becomes overheated and cannot eliminate this excess heat, heat exhaustion and heat stroke are possible.

Heat exhaustion is generally characterized by clammy skin, fatigue, nausea, dizziness, profuse perspiration, and sometimes fainting, resulting from an inadequate intake of water and the loss of fluids. First aid treatment for this condition includes having the victim lie down, raising the feet 8–12 inches, applying cool, wet cloths to the skin, and giving the victim sips of salt water (1 teaspoon per glass, half a glass every 15 minutes), over the period of an hour.

Heat stroke is much more serious; it is an immediate life-threatening situation. The characteristics of heat stroke are a high body temperature (which may reach 106°F or more); a rapid pulse; hot, dry skin; and a blocked sweating mechanism. Victims of this condition may be unconscious, and first aid measures should be directed at cooling the body quickly. The victim should be placed in a tub of cold water or repeatedly sponged with cool water until his or her temperature is lowered sufficiently. Fans or air conditioners will also help with the cooling process. Care should be taken, however, not to over-chill the victim once the temperature is below 102°F.

76. The most immediate concern of a person tending a victim of heat stroke should be to

a. get salt into the victim's body
b. raise the victim's feet
c. lower the victim's pulse
d. lower the victim's temperature

77. Which of the following is a symptom of heat exhaustion?

a. unconsciousness
b. profuse sweating
c. hot, dry skin
d. a weak pulse

78. Heat stroke is more serious than heat exhaustion because heat stroke victims

a. do not sweat
b. have no salt in their bodies
c. cannot take in water
d. have frequent fainting spells

79. Symptoms such as nausea and dizziness in a heat exhaustion victim indicates that the person most likely needs to

a. be immediately taken to a hospital
b. be given more salt water
c. be immersed in a tub of water
d. sweat more

SET 10 (Answers begin on page 154.)

As you read, try identifying the author's *motive* for writing the passage. This will be especially helpful when asked to choose the best title for the passage. Is the author's purpose to inform you of facts? Persuade you of something? Simply entertain you?

Although more and more people are exercising regularly, experts note that eating right is also a key to good health. Nutritionists recommend the "food pyramid" for a simple guide to eating the proper foods. At the base of the food pyramid are grains and fiber. You should eat six to eleven servings of bread, cereal, rice, and pasta everyday. Next up the pyramid are vegetables and fruit; five to nine daily servings from this group are recommended. The next pyramid level is the dairy group. Two or three servings a day of milk, yogurt, or cheese help maintain good nutrition. Moving up the pyramid, the next level is the meat, poultry, fish, beans, eggs, and nuts group, of which everyone should eat only two to three servings a day. At the very top of the pyramid are fats, oils and sweets; these foods should be eaten only infrequently.

You don't have to shop in health food stores to follow the guidelines. One easy way to plan menus that follow the food pyramid is to shop only in the outer aisles of the grocery store. In most supermarkets, fresh fruit and vegetables, dairy, fresh meat and frozen foods are in the outer aisles of the store. Grains, like pasta, rice, bread, and cereal, are located on the next aisles, the first inner rows. Finally, the farthest inside of the store is where you'll find chips and snacks, cookies and pastries, soda pop and drink mixes. These are the kinds of foods that nutritionists say everyone should eat rarely, if at all. If you stay in the outer aisles of the grocery store, you won't be tempted to buy foods you shouldn't eat, and you will find a wide variety of healthy foods to choose from. Another benefit of shopping this way is that grocery shopping takes less time.

80. A good title for this article would be
a. How to Shop in a Health Food Store
b. How to Shop Efficiently
c. How to Shop for Healthy Food
d. How to Cook Healthy Food

81. According to the passage, the best way to shop in the grocery store is to
a. make a list and stick to it
b. stay in the outside aisles
c. stay in the inside aisles
d. check the newspaper ads for bargains

82. According to the food pyramid, people should
a. eat more grains than meat
b. never eat fats and sweets
c. eat mostly vegetarian meals
d. rarely eat bread and other starches

83. According to the passage, on the inside aisles of the grocery store you will find
a. cleaning products
b. dog and cat food
c. wine and beer
d. chips and snacks

84. According to the passage, to maintain good health, people should
a. buy their food in health food stores
b. worry more about nutrition than exercise
c. exercise and eat right
d. eat from the top of the food pyramid

85. In order to follow the main advice in the passage, it would be most helpful to know
a. where to purchase a copy of "The Food Pyramid"
b. whether rice has more calories than pasta
c. which supermarket the author is referring to
d. how much of each kind of food equals a serving

SET 11 (Answers begin on page 154.)

On almost any job you get, you'll be asked to read policy, work instructions, and rules. Following are a number of job-related passages. Start with these relatively simple notices posted for workers.

Notice

All drivers are responsible for refueling their taxicabs at the end of each shift. All other routine maintenance is performed by maintenance department personnel, who are also responsible for maintaining service records. If a worker believes a taxicab is in need of mechanical repair, she or he should fill out the pink "Repair Requisition" form and turn it in to the shift supervisor. The worker should also notify the shift supervisor verbally whether, in the worker's opinion, the taxicab must be repaired immediately or may be driven for the rest of the shift.

86. If a taxicab is due to have the oil changed, whose responsibility is it?
  a. maintenance department personnel
  b. the drivers at the end of their shifts
  c. shift supervisors
  d. outside service mechanics

87. The passage implies that the taxicabs
  a. are refueled when they have less than half a tank of gas
  b. have the oil changed every 1,000 miles
  c. are refueled at the end of every shift
  d. are in frequent need of repair

Notice

Beginning next month, the city will institute a program intended to remove the graffiti from city-owned delivery trucks. Any truck that finishes its assigned route before the end of the driver's shift will return to its lot where supervisors will provide materials for that driver to use in cleaning the truck. Because the length of time it takes to complete different tasks and routes vary, trucks within the same department will no longer be assigned to specific routes but will be rotated among the routes. Therefore, workers should no longer leave personal items in the trucks, as they will not necessarily be driving the same truck each day as in the past.

88. According to the passage, the removal of graffiti from trucks will be done by
  a. a small group of drivers specifically assigned to the task
  b. custodians who work for the city
  c. any supervisor or driver who finishes a route first
  d. each driver as that driver finishes his or her route

89. According to the passage, routes within particular departments
  a. vary in the amount of time they take to complete
  b. vary in the amount of graffiti they're likely to have on them
  c. are all of approximately equal length
  d. vary according to the truck's driver

90. According to the passage, prior to instituting the graffiti clean-up program, city workers
  a. were not responsible for cleaning the trucks
  b. had to re-paint the trucks at intervals
  c. usually drove the same truck each workday
  d. were not allowed to leave personal belongings in the trucks

Memo to Supervisory Personnel

Members of your investigative team may have skills and abilities that you are not aware of. As investigator in charge of a case, you should seek out and take advantage of potential talent in all the members of your team. Whenever a new case is given to your team, it is usually a good idea to have all the members come up with ideas and suggestions about all aspects of the case, rather than insisting that each member stick rigidly to his or her narrow area of expertise. This way, you are likely to discover special investigative skills you never suspected your team members had. It's worthwhile to take extra time to explore all your team's talents.

91. The paragraph best supports the statement that a single member of an investigative team

a. may have abilities that the leader of the team doesn't know about
b. usually stands out as having more ideas that other members do
c. should be assigned the task of discovering the whole team's talents
d. can have more skills and abilities than all the rest

All Drivers Take Note

The City Transit supervisors have received numerous complaints over the last several weeks about buses on several routes running hot. Drivers are reminded that each route has several check points at which drivers should check the time. If the bus is ahead of schedule, drivers should delay at the check point until it is the proper time to leave. If traffic makes it unsafe for a driver to delay at a particular check point, the driver should proceed at a reasonable speed to the next stop and hold there until the bus is back on schedule.

92. According to the passage, when a bus is "running hot" it means

a. the bus is going too fast and the engine is over-heating
b. the bus is running ahead of schedule
c. the bus is running behind schedule
d. passengers are complaining about the bus being off schedule

93. The main point of the passage is that drivers should

a. stop their buses when traffic is unsafe
b. drive at a reasonable speed
c. check the time at every stop
d. see that their buses run on schedule

SET 12 (Answers begin on page 154.)

Here are more job-related notices. Continue to read closely and carefully, keeping in mind that skimming can lead to mistakes.

Important Warning

Only supervisors of the Sanitation Department are qualified to handle hazardous waste. Hazardous waste is defined as any waste designated by the United States Environmental Protection Agency as hazardous. If you are unclear whether a particular item is hazardous, you should not handle the item but should instead notify the supervisor for directions.

94. Hazardous waste is defined as

a. anything too dangerous for sanitation workers to handle
b. waste picked up by special sanitation trucks
c. anything so designated by the United States Environmental Protection Agency
d. waste not allowed to be placed alongside regular residential garbage

95. Sanitation Worker Harris comes upon a container of cleaning solvent along with the regular garbage in front of a residence. The container does not list the contents of the cleaner; therefore, according to the directions, Harris should

a. assume the solvent is safe and deposit it in the sanitation truck
b. leave a note for the residents, asking them to list the contents of the solvent
c. simply leave the container on the curb
d. contact the supervisor for directions

Notice of Mandatory Refresher Training Course

During the next ten months, all bus operators with two or more years of service will be required to have completed twenty hours of refresher training on one of the Vehicle Maneuvering Training Buses.

Instructors who have used this new technology report that trainees develop skills more quickly than with traditional training methods. In refresher training, this new system reinforces defensive driving skills and safe driving habits. Drivers can also check their reaction times and hand-eye coordination.

As an added side benefit, the city expects to save money with the simulators because the new system reduces the amount of training time in an actual bus, saving on parts, fuel, and other operating expenses.

96. All bus operators are required to do which of the following?

a. receive training in defensive driving and operating a computer
b. complete ten months of refresher driver training
c. train new drivers on how to operate a simulator
d. complete twenty hours of training on a simulator

97. The main purpose of the refresher training course on the simulator is to

a. make sure that all bus operators are maintaining proper driving habits
b. give experienced bus operators an opportunity to learn new driving techniques
c. help all bus operators to develop hand-eye coordination
d. reduce the city's operating budget

Notice: Training to Begin for F.A.S.T. Membership

A training calendar and schedule for F.A.S.T. membership is available in this office to all applicants for F.A.S.T. membership. Training will take place the third week of each month. Classes will be taught on Monday afternoons, Wednesday evenings, and Saturday afternoons.

So that the Fire Agency Specialties Team (F.A.S.T.) can maintain a high level of efficiency and preparedness for emergency response situations, its members must meet certain requirements.

First, in order for you to be considered for membership on F.A.S.T., your department must be a member of the F.A.S.T. organization, and you must have written permission from your fire chief or your department's highest ranking administrator.

Once active, you must meet further requirements to maintain active status. These include completion of technician level training and certification in hazardous material (hazmat) operations. In addition, after becoming a member, you must also attend a minimum of 50 percent of all drills conducted by F.A.S.T. and go to at least one F.A.S.T. conference. You may qualify for alternative credit for drills by proving previous experience in actual hazmat emergency response.

If you fail to meet minimum requirements you will be considered inactive, and the director of your team will be notified. You will be placed back on active status only after you complete the training necessary to meet the minimum requirements.

98. Potential F.A.S.T. members can attend less than half of F.A.S.T. drills if they
- a. complete technician level training requirements
- b. indicate prior real emergency experience
- c. receive permission from their fire chief
- d. enroll in three weekly training sessions

99. Which of the following is the main subject of the passage?
- a. preparing for hazmat certification
- b. the main goal of F.A.S.T.
- c. completing F.A.S.T. membership requirements
- d. learning about your department's F.A.S.T. membership

100. Applicants must be available for training
- a. three days each month
- b. three days each week
- c. every third month
- d. for fifty percent of classes

SET 13 (Answers begin on page 154.)

This set contains two job-related definitions. See if you can apply them to the job situations described in the questions that follow them.

Criminal Simulation occurs when, with intent to defraud or harm another, a person alters an object so that it appears to have more worth than it has because of age, antiquity, rarity, or authorship.

101. Which situation below is the best example of Criminal Simulation?

a. Bess Rossburg sews an American flag from scratch and enters it in a contest using the name Betsy Ross.

b. On Elvis' birthday, Eric dresses up as an Elvis look-alike and sells blue velvet paintings of the singer on a street corner.

c. Edith writes a poem onto a scrap of ancient paper, signs it Edna St. Vincent Milay, and sells it to an antique dealer.

d. Wendell finds an old ship's bell in a navy surplus store and tells his friends he got it from one of the men who helped recover the Titanic a few years ago.

Harassment occurs when one person, with the intention of annoying, alarming, or tormenting another person, threatens—by telephone or in writing—to harm that person, damage his or her property, or harm a member of his or her family.

102. Which situation below is the best example of Harassment?

a. Lydia leaves a note on Pete's car telling him that she didn't like it when he asked her out on a date and that she'll call police if he ever asks again.

b. Rudy calls Edward on the phone and tells him he is going to break out the headlights on Edward's car if he doesn't stop parking in front of Rudy's house.

c. Tyler calls a jealous husband, Ramon, and tells him he is dating Ramon's ex-wife.

d. Armando writes a note to Julia telling her that, because she is 6 months behind on her rent, he is going to padlock her doors.

SET 14 (Answers begin on page 154.)

The next few sets describe on-the-job situations that police officers might face. In order to arrive at the answers to the questions, first read closely, then make notes of important explicit facts.

Police Officer Maxwell has been told by residents in his patrol area that thefts are on the rise. Car thefts take place primarily on Moray Street between Elm and Chestnut Avenues. Most of the jewelry thefts take place on Elm Avenue between George and Larson Streets. Most of the thefts of electronic equipment take place on Deiner Street between Chestnut and Maple Avenues. Electronic equipment thefts tend to take place on Mondays and Fridays. Car thefts often take place on Saturdays and Wednesdays. Most jewelry thefts take place on Thursdays and Sundays. Jewelry thefts usually occur between 1:00 p.m. and 3:00 p.m., electronic equipment thefts between 4:00 p.m. and 8:00 p.m., and car thefts between midnight and 3:00 a.m.

103. Officer Maxwell would be most effective in reducing the number of thefts of electronic equipment if he patrolled from

a. 1:00 p.m. to 9:00 p.m., Friday through Tuesday

b. 8:00 p.m. to 4:00 a.m., Monday through Friday

c. midnight to 8:00 a.m., Wednesday through Sunday

d. noon to 8:00 p.m., Tuesday through Saturday

104. Residents of the area are particularly concerned about the car thefts. If Officer Maxwell wants to reduce the number of car thefts, he should patrol

a. Deiner Street between Chestnut and Maple Avenues on Thursdays and Sundays between 1:00 p.m. and 4:00 p.m.

b. Moray Street between Elm and Chestnut Avenues on Wednesdays and Saturdays between 10:00 p.m. and 4:00 a.m.

c. Elm Avenue between George and Larson Streets on Mondays and Fridays between midnight and 6:00 a.m.

d. Moray Street between Maple and Chestnut Avenues on Saturdays and Wednesdays between 7:00 p.m. and 1:00 a.m.

Police Officer Alvarez has noticed an increase in violent crimes in the area she patrols. She has noticed that robberies at gunpoint seem to be concentrated on First Avenue between Eleventh and Twelfth Streets. Most rapes take place on Second Avenue between Twelfth and Fourteenth Streets. Almost all of the assaults take place on Fourteenth Street between Second and Third Avenues. Most rapes take place on Fridays and Saturdays; assaults occur on Mondays and Thursdays; robberies at gunpoint take place on Sundays and Wednesdays. Assaults most often take place between 11:00 p.m. and 2:00 a.m., robberies at gunpoint between 6:00 p.m. and 8:00 p.m., and rapes between 9:00 p.m. and 11:00 p.m.

105. In order to reduce the number of robberies at gunpoint, Officer Alvarez should patrol the area

a. along First Avenue between Eleventh and Twelfth Streets on Mondays and Thursdays between 6:00 p.m. and 11:00 a.m.
b. between Second and Third Avenues on Sundays and Wednesdays between 6:00 p.m. and 8:00 p.m. on Fourteenth Street
c. between Twelfth and Eleventh Streets along First Avenue, on Sundays and Wednesdays between 6:00 p.m. and midnight.
d. along Second Avenue between Fourteenth and Twelfth Streets on Fridays and Saturdays between 5:00 p.m. and 11:00 p.m.

SET 15 (Answers begin on page 155.)

Remember to read the entire passage closely before extracting bare-bones facts. Don't forget to ask the questions, Who? What? When? Where? How? and Why? When the participants in these crime-related incidents make statements, ask yourself, "Is that a fact or an opinion? Is it possibly a distortion of truth or even a lie?"

At 1:30 a.m., while parked at 917 Crescent, Police Officers Lin and Lawton were asked to respond to a call from Tucker's Tavern at 714 Clarinda. At 1:42 a.m., when the officers arrived, they found paramedics attempting to revive 18-year-old Brent Morrow, who lay unconscious on the floor. A patron of the tavern, Edward Pickens, stated that at around 12:10 a.m., Mr. Morrow's two companions had playfully challenged Mr. Morrow to "chug" a pint of whiskey and that Mr. Morrow had done so in approximately 15 minutes. Mr. Pickens thought the two should be arrested. Mr. Morrow's companions, Jeremy Roland and Casey Edwards, denied Mr. Pickens' statement. The bartender, Raymond Evans, stated he had not served Mr. Morrow and that Tucker's Tavern does not sell whiskey by the pint. At 1:50 a.m. paramedics took Mr. Morrow to University Hospital where he remains unconscious. No arrests were made. An investigation is pending.

106. Which of the following persons most likely called police to Tucker's Tavern?
a. Raymond Evans
b. Brent Morrow
c. Jeremy Roland
d. Edward Pickens

107. What was the main reason Brent Morrow was removed from Tucker's Tavern?
a. He was drunk.
b. He was under-age.
c. He was ill.
d. He was a university student.

108. What is the most likely reason Brent Morrow's companions challenged him to chug a pint of whiskey?
a. They thought it would be fun.
b. They wanted him to get sick.
c. They thought it was time he "grew up."
d. They were trying to get even with him.

109. At about what time did Brent Morrow finish chugging the pint of whiskey?
a. 12:25 a.m.
b. 1:30 a.m.
c. 1:42 a.m.
d. 1:50 a.m.

At 12:15 a.m., while riding the uptown-bound 12 subway, Transit Officers Cobb and Wilson received a report of a disturbance in the fourth car of a downtown-bound 12 train. That train was held at the Fourth Street station until the arrival of the officers, who found complainant Alan Sterns tending his injured eye. Mr. Sterns told Officer Wilson he had been attacked by Caroline Simpson when he attempted to move her bags, after politely asking her to do so, in order to make room to sit down. He said Miss Simpson poked him in the eye, then threatened him with a switchblade. Miss Simpson told Officer Cobb she had been harassed by Mr. Sterns and struck him in self-defense. The officers asked Mr. Sterns, Miss Simpson, and witnesses Lisa Walker and Lois Casey to step off the train and proceeded to question them on the platform. Miss Walker, whose view was partially obstructed by a metal pole, stated that Mr. Sterns had only raised his arm after being struck, but she was not sure whether the gesture was threatening or defensive. Miss Casey, who sat on the other side of Miss Simpson, maintained that Mr. Sterns was only protecting himself and had behaved in a polite manner. Miss Simpson was placed under arrest for carrying a concealed weapon.

110. Where did the assault occur?
  a. on a subway platform
  b. on the fourth car of the uptown-bound 12 train
  c. at the Fourth Street station
  d. on the downtown-bound 12 train

111. Which of the following actions caused the arrest?
  a. injuring the complainant's eye
  b. threatening the complainant
  c. carrying a switchblade
  d. disturbing the peace

112. The complainant's last name is
  a. Sterns
  b. Simpson
  c. Walker
  d. Cobb

113. Where was Miss Casey sitting?
  a. beside the complainant
  b. across the car, behind a metal pole
  c. between the complainant and the accused
  d. beside the accused

114. According to the complainant, he was struck because
  a. he handled the woman's property
  b. he asked the woman to move her bags
  c. he politely asked the woman to move over
  d. he appeared to raise his arm in a threatening manner

SET 16 (Answers begin on page 155.)

The reading process is the same no matter what kind of job-related material you're confronted with. Read carefully so as not to miss some small but crucial detail. Don't skim. Make lists.

At 9:30 p.m., while parked at 916 Woodward Avenue, Police Officers Whitebear and Morgan were asked to respond to an anonymous complaint of a disturbance at 826 Rosemary Lane. When they arrived, they found the back door open and the jamb splintered. They drew their weapons, identified themselves, and entered the dwelling, where they found Mr. Darrell Hensley, of 1917 Roosevelt Avenue, sitting on the couch. Mr. Hensley calmly stated he was waiting for his wife. At that point, two children emerged from a hallway: Dustin Hensley, age 7, who lives in the dwelling; and Kirstin Jackson, age 14, Dustin's baby-sitter, who lives at 916 Ambrose Street. Kirstin stated she and Dustin had been sitting at the kitchen table when the back door was kicked in and Mr. Hensley entered, shouting obscenities and calling for Karen Hensley, Dustin's mother. Kirstin then hid with Dustin in a hallway storage closet. The officers contacted Mrs. Hensley at her place of employment at O'Reilley's Restaurant at 415 Ralston. At 9:55 she returned home and showed an Order of Protection stating Mr. Hensley was not to have contact with his wife or child. Mr. Hensley was placed under arrest and taken in handcuffs to the station house.

115. Based on Darrell Hensley's behavior when he first arrived at his wife's house, what was his most likely motivation for being there?

a. to see his child, whom he loved
b. to force his wife to deal with him
c. to have a place to stay that night
d. to peacefully reconcile with his family

116. Who called the police to investigate the disturbance described in the passage?

a. the baby-sitter
b. the arrestee's wife
c. a neighbor
d. an unknown person

117. Based on the information in the passage, what is the most likely reason the officers drew their weapons before entering the Hensley home?

a. There were signs of forced entry into the house.
b. There was an Order of Protection against Mr. Hensley.
c. Children were in danger inside the premises.
d. They knew Mr. Hensley to be a violent man.

118. Based on the information in the passage, what was Mr. Hensley's demeanor when the police first spoke to him?

a. He was enraged.
b. He was remorseful.
c. He was matter-of-fact.
d. He was confused.

SET 17 (Answers begin on page 155.)

Remember that active reading is the first step to comprehension. For these police-work-related incidents, underline or write down the names of the persons involved, the place where the main incident happened, the time of the incident, and the actions of the participants.

At 2:15 a.m., while parked at 7238 Los Feliz Boulevard, Police Officers Sloane and Rosas observed a gold Chevrolet Corsica, license number XZQ419, run a red light while doing 35 in a 25-mile-per-hour zone. The officers went in pursuit and pulled the Corsica over in front of 4819 Los Feliz Boulevard. The driver, Raul Hernandez, a juvenile, was unable to produce a license, and the car was registered to Hector Herrera, of 2112 Los Feliz Boulevard, apartment 3B. Mr. Hernandez claimed the vehicle's owner was his stepfather. After passing a sobriety test, Mr. Hernandez was handcuffed by Officer Rosas and placed under arrest. At the station, Officer Rosas telephoned Mr. Herrera, who confirmed that he was married to Mr. Hernandez's mother. He stated that Raul was in the custody of his father, Frank Hernandez, 122 Whitney Boulevard. Raul stated that he used his key to his mother's house to obtain entry, found the keys on the kitchen counter, and took the car without permission. Mr. Herrera requested that auto theft charges be brought against the boy. As the boy seemed to be in the act of returning the car, he was charged with joyriding, as well as the other moving violations.

119. Where does Raul Hernandez live?

a. 4819 Los Feliz Boulevard
b. 122 Whitney Boulevard
c. 7238 Los Feliz Boulevard
d. 2112 Los Feliz Boulevard

120. Which of the following is a complete list of Raul Hernandez's moving violations?

a. driving while intoxicated, reckless driving, running a red light
b. auto theft, reckless driving, running a red light
c. joyriding, driving without a license, speeding, running a red light
d. joyriding, driving without a license, driving while intoxicated, speeding, running a red light

121. Who wants Raul to be charged with auto theft?

a. Mr. Whitney
b. Mr. Hernandez
c. Mr. Herrera
d. Mr. Rosas

At 3:15 p.m., while parked in front of 761 Marcy Avenue, Police Officers Walters and Johnson received a radio call of a prowler in the back yard of a house at 213 Winston Street. The radio dispatcher informed the officers that the call came from William Gale, of 216 Winston Street. The officers found no intruder or sign of forcible entry at the scene. Officer Johnson questioned Mr. Gale, who reported noticing a man sitting in a van in front of his house for over an hour before crossing the street and entering the back yard of Mr. Gale's neighbor, Eleanor Stern. Mr. Gale stated that after he called the police, the man returned to his van and left. He gave the officers the license plate number, VXY117. As the officers returned to their patrol car, the van in question turned onto Winston Street. The officers flagged it over. The driver was identified as Arthur Macy. Mr. Macy admitted to trespassing, but claimed to be searching for his dog, which was now in the van. The officers radioed for a check on Mr. Macy. On discovering there was an Order of Protection that stated that Mr. Macy was to stay away from Miss Stern and her residence the officers placed Mr. Macy under arrest.

122. Which of the following alerted the police to the intruder?

a. Mr. Gale
b. Mr. Marcy
c. Mr. Stern
d. Mr. Johnson

123. The suspect was reported trespassing at

a. 761 Marcy Avenue
b. 216 Winston Street
c. 716 Marcy Avenue
d. 213 Winston Street

124. Which of the following actions caused Mr. Macy to be arrested?

a. suspicious behavior
b. theft
c. violating an Order of Protection
d. forced entry

SET 18 (Answers begin on page 156.)

For this set try answering the following questions: Which details comprise the facts of the case? Which are merely the participants' opinions? Being able to separate fact from opinion is essential to reading comprehension.

At 12:45 a.m. on October 15, while parked at 1910 Fairlane, Police Officers Flores and Steinbrenner were asked to respond to a disturbance at 1809 Clarkson. When they arrived at the one-story dwelling, the complainant, Alan Weber, who resides next door at 1807 Clarkson, told them that he had been kept awake for two hours by the sound of yelling and breaking glass. He said the occupant of 1809 Clarkson, a Mr. Everett Hayes, lived alone, was crazy, and had always been crazy. As they approached the house, they heard yelling coming from inside. When the officers knocked on the door, Mr. Hayes answered promptly and said, "It's about time you got here." Inside, broken furniture was strewn about. Mr. Hayes stated he had been protecting himself from persons who lived inside the woodwork of his home. He went willingly with the officers to Fairfield County Hospital at 1010 Market, where he was admitted to the psychiatric unit for observation. No arrests were made.

125. Which of the following is most likely a fact?
a. Alan Weber had been kept awake by noise.
b. Mr. Hayes had been making noise for two hours.
c. Mr. Hayes had always been crazy.
d. The police heard Mr. Hayes shouting inside his house.

126. The call to the police was most likely made from which of the following addresses?
a. 1910 Fairlane
b. 1809 Clarkson
c. 1807 Clarkson
d. 1010 Market

127. Based on the passage, what was the most likely reason the police were called?
a. A neighbor was bothered by the noise coming from Mr. Hayes' home.
b. A neighbor was worried for Mr. Hayes' safety.
c. A neighbor was worried for the safety of Mr. Hayes' family.
d. A neighbor was curious about Mr. Hayes' personal life.

128. What was Mr. Hayes' demeanor when the police arrived at his door?
a. He seemed surprised.
b. He seemed to have been expecting them.
c. He seemed frightened and distrustful.
d. He seemed angered by their presence.

129. Based on the passage, what reason would Mr. Hayes himself most likely give for the commotion at his house?
a. He was acting in self-defense.
b. He was mentally ill.
c. He was cleaning the woodwork.
d. He was annoyed at his neighbors.

At 9:20 a.m., Officers Torres and Verona investigated a burglary at 212 Hawkins Drive, Apartment 2107. Robert Larkin reported that he left for work at 10 p.m. and returned at 8:15 a.m. to find his television, VCR, CD player, and several CDs missing. After calling the police, he reported hearing music coming through the ceiling and stated that he suspected his upstairs neighbor, Lawrence Cole, who lives in Apartment 3107. Mr. Larkin stated that Mr. Cole had a key to Mr. Larkin's apartment and that there was no sign of forced entry. Further, he said that Mr. Cole had not previously owned a CD player. Mr. Larkin reported that the two had recently had a falling out. The officers questioned Mr. Cole, who claimed that he had been at the apartment of his girlfriend, Terri Fork, 210 Hawkins Drive, Apartment 3112, from 9:30 p.m. until 8:30 a.m. Ms. Fork confirmed this. Mr. Larkin could not produce receipts for the merchandise in question, save for the CD player. The receipt supported Mr. Larkin's claim that he purchased the CD player from his neighbor, Irene Franklin, in Apartment 3218. The serial numbers on the CD player were filed off. Ms. Franklin could not be located, and the officers decided to investigate further.

130. Who reported the crime?
- a. a neighbor
- b. the suspect
- c. the victim
- d. the suspect's girlfriend

131. Where does the suspect's girlfriend live?
- a. 212 Hawkins Drive, Apartment 3107
- b. 212 Hawkins Drive, Apartment 3218
- c. 210 Hawkins Drive, Apartment 3218
- d. 210 Hawkins Drive, Apartment 3112

132. Who failed to produce a receipt for the VCR?
- a. Mr. Larkin
- b. Ms. Franklin
- c. Ms. Fork
- d. Mr. Cole

133. Who may have been in possession of stolen merchandise?
- a. the victim
- b. the suspect and the neighbor
- c. the neighbor
- d. the suspect, the victim, and the neighbor

134. When did the burglary take place?
- a. approximately 9:20 a.m.
- b. between 8:15 p.m. and 9:20 a.m.
- c. approximately 9:30 p.m.
- d. between 10:00 p.m. and 8:15 a.m.

SET 19 (Answers begin on page 156.)

One strategy for improving your reading skill is to be aware of the *structure* of the piece of writing you're working with, its organizational pattern. Four main patterns are: chronological order, hierarchical order (order of importance, most-to-least, least-to-most), comparison-contrast, and cause-and-effect. Another way to organize material is simply by topic. The next few sets present instructions that pertain to police and firefighter work. Try your hand at identifying the organizational scheme behind each one.

After a fire is put out, the firefighter must routinely write a report on what occurred at the scene. This is normally done back at the firehouse on a computer in the following manner:

1. Log on to the computer.
2. Go to the directory that contains the report forms.
3. If there was a death on the scene, complete report form 111.
4. If there were injuries on the scene, complete report form 103.
5. If there was loss of or damage to equipment, complete form 107.
6. If there was no injury, death, equipment loss, or equipment damage, complete form 101.
7. If form 107 *and* form 103 are required, complete form 122 also.
8. Complete form 106, which is a general report and must be filled out for *all* fire reports.
9. Print and file all forms that have been completed, and fax a copy to division headquarters.

135. Which of the following organizational schemes is the main one used in the list of instructions?
a. order of importance
b. cause-and-effect
c. chronological order
d. organization by topic

136. A firefighter has just returned to the firehouse after a fire and is preparing the necessary report forms. One of the residents of the house that burned was injured and sent to the hospital. Also, one of the fire hoses was damaged. There were no deaths at the fire. Which forms must the firefighter complete?
a. forms 101 and 106
b. forms 111 and 107
c. forms 103, 106, 107, and 122
d. forms 106, 111, and 122

137. A firefighter is filling out fire reports on a fire in which there was one death, no equipment damage or loss, and one injury in addition to the death. Which forms must the firefighter complete?
a. forms 103, 106, and 122
b. forms 103 and 111
c. forms 101, 106, and 122
d. forms 103, 106, and 111

138. A firefighter is preparing a report on a grass fire that was put out with no injuries, no deaths, and no equipment damage or loss. Which form must the firefighter complete?
a. form 106
b. form 111
c. form 107
d. form 103

SET 20 (Answers begin on page 156.)

Again, Identifying the organization of a block of text can often make its meaning more clear. Consider the organizational pattern behind this set of firefighter-related instructions, for example.

The Fire Department has issued a notice stating that the preferred order for removal of civilians from a fire building is as follows:

1. Interior stairs
2. Adjoining building
3. Fire escape
4. Ladder
5. Roof rescue rope
6. Life net

139. Which of the following organizational schemes does the above list of instructions follow?
a. hierarchical order
b. chronological order
c. order by topic
d. comparison-contrast

140. Which of the following is the best means of removing fire victims from a burning building?
a. leading them down a fire escape
b. using the aerial ladder or tower ladder
c. using the stairway inside the building
d. using a life net

141. What means of saving civilians trapped by fire would be used only as a last resort?
a. using a roof rescue rope and removing the victims through a window
b. taking them out via an adjoining building
c. telling them to jump into the life net
d. raising a portable ladder to a window

142. Several firefighters suddenly become trapped by the fire they are fighting. They cannot get out by the interior stairs or through the adjoining building. What method of escape should they try next?
a. the fire escape
b. a ladder
c. the roof rescue rope
d. the life net

143. Before resorting to using the ladder, a firefighter should try all the following escape methods, EXCEPT
a. going through the adjoining building
b. sliding down the roof rescue rope
c. using the interior stairs
d. using the fire escape

QUESTIONS

A firefighter's self-contained breathing apparatus must be inspected at the beginning of each tour and after each use. The following procedure is used to ensure that a thorough inspection is completed.

1. Check the condition of the harness assembly. The harness assembly should be free of defects. If defects are found, the unit should be placed out of service.
2. Check the condition of the air cylinder, and read the cylinder gauge. If the cylinder is damaged or less than full, it must be replaced.
3. Turn the air cylinder on.
4. Examine the hoses and hose couplings. Check for cuts or air leaks. If any are found, the unit must be placed out of service.
5. Inspect the face piece and regulator. If either is found to be damaged, the unit must be placed out of service.
6. Test the system. Don the face piece, and inhale and exhale to verify that the system is functioning. Malfunctioning units must be placed out of service.
7. Shut down the unit.

144. Which of the following organizational scheme does the above list of instructions follow?

a. hierarchical order
b. order by topic
c. cause-and-effect
d. chronological order

145. The self-contained breathing apparatus must be inspected

a. weekly
b. only after use
c. before each tour and after it is used
d. before each use

146. The cylinder gauge on the breathing apparatus you are inspecting reads half-full. You should

a. place the unit out of service
b. replace the cylinder with a full one
c. use the cylinder until it is empty
d. turn the air cylinder on

147. The air cylinder should be turned on

a. before the inspection is begun
b. after checking the condition of the hose coupling
c. after checking the cylinder gauge
d. after the inspection is complete

SET 21 (Answers begin on page 157.)

This set of instructions pertains to police work. Again, begin by noting the structure or organizational pattern of the passages. Then move on to underlining or taking notes on important points.

The Advisory Committee of the State Police have issued the following Guidelines for establishing a roadblock in order to identify and apprehend drunk drivers:

1. Selecting the location. The roadblock must be established in a location that affords motorists a clear view of the stop. It cannot be established, for example, just over a hill or around a curve. Motorists must be able to see that a roadblock is ahead and that cars are being stopped.

2. Staffing the location. A roadblock must display visible signs of police authority. Therefore, uniformed officers in marked patrol cars should primarily staff the roadblock. Plain-clothes officers may supplement the staff at a roadblock, but the initial stop and questioning of motorists should be conducted by uniformed officers. In addition to the officers conducting the motorist stops, officers should be present to conduct field sobriety tests on suspect drivers. A command observation officer must also be present to coordinate the roadblock.

3. Operating the roadblock. All cars passing through the roadblock must be stopped. It should not appear to an approaching motorist that cars are being singled out for some reason while others are not stopped, as this will generate unnecessary fear on the part of the motorist. The observation vehicle which is present at the roadblock will be able to pursue any motorists that refuse to stop.

4. Questioning the drivers. Each motorist stopped by the roadblock should be questioned only briefly. In most cases, an officer should ask directly if the driver has been drinking. In suspicious cases, an officer may engage in some further questioning to allow her or him to evaluate the driver's sobriety. A driver who appears to have been drinking should be directed to the side of the road, out of the line of traffic, where other officers may conduct a field sobriety test. Each non-suspicious driver should be stopped only briefly, for approximately a minute or less.

5. Duration of operation. No drunk-driving roadblock should be in operation for more than two hours. Roadblocks in place for longer periods lose their effectiveness as word spreads as to the location of the roadblock, and motorists who have been drinking will avoid the area. In addition, on average only about one percent of all the drivers who pass through a roadblock will be arrested for drunk-driving, and, after a short period of time, officers can be used more efficiently elsewhere.

6. Charges other than drunk-driving. A roadblock may only be established for a single purpose—in this case, detecting drunk drivers—and should not be seen as an opportunity to check for a variety of motorist offenses. However, officers are not required to ignore what is plainly obvious. For example, motorists and passengers who are not wearing seat belts should be verbally warned that failure to do so is against the law. Detaining and ticketing such drivers is not the purpose of the roadblock and would unduly slow down the stops of other cars. An officer who spots a situation that presents a clear and present danger should follow through by directing the motorist to the side of the road where the officers are conducting field sobriety tests. These officers can then follow through on investigating the driver for crimes other than drunk-driving.

148. Which organizational pattern do the Guidelines follow?

a. hierarchical order
b. chronological order
c. cause-and-effect
d. comparison-contrast

149. According to the Guidelines, officers must make sure they set up a drunk-driving roadblock that

a. can be seen by motorists from a distance
b. provides a well-hidden place for officers to park their cars
c. is near a bar or tavern
d. is near a busy street or highway

150. While questioning motorists at a drunk-driving roadblock, Officer Firth notices that, although the driver of a particular car appears to be sober, the passenger in that car seems extremely nervous and has bruises on his face. She asks the passenger if he is all right and, after glancing at the driver, the passenger nods, "yes." According to the Guidelines, Officer Firth should:

a. let the car pass through, because the driver is not drunk
b. question the passenger and driver further about the passenger's condition
c. arrest the driver on suspicion of assault
d. direct the driver to pull to the side of the road where other officers can investigate further

151. Officers have been conducting a drunk-driving roadblock since 7:00 p.m. and have made 35 drunk-driving arrests, which is one-quarter of all cars stopped. It is now 9:00 p.m. According to the Guidelines, the officers should:

a. continue the roadblock because they are making a high percentage of arrests
b. re-establish the roadblock one-quarter mile down the road
c. dismantle the roadblock, because it has been in operation for two hours
d. ask the Advisory Committee for permission to operate the roadblock longer

152. Officers have been directed to operate a drunk-driving roadblock from 6:00 p.m. to 8:00 p.m. at the corner of Greene and First. At 6:45, the unusually heavy traffic begins to back up. According to the Guidelines, officers should not

a. dismantle the roadblock early
b. begin stopping only every third car
c. move the roadblock to a quieter intersection
d. ask for extra officers to help staff the roadblock

153. According to the Guidelines, the officers stopping and questioning motorists at a drunk-driving roadblock should be in uniform so that motorists

a. will take the roadblock more seriously
b. will answer their questions more truthfully
c. can identify which agency they are from
d. can tell from a distance that this is an official activity

154. Officer Robb is stopping and questioning eastbound cars at the drunk-driving roadblock on Highway 7. He asks one driver if she has been drinking. The driver says, "No, Officer, I haven't," but she slurs her words. According to the Guidelines, Officer Robb should:

a. ask the driver a couple more questions
b. arrest the driver for drunk driving
c. ask the driver to take a breathalyzer test
d. pass the driver through with a warning

155. A car approaching a drunk-driving roadblock slows down, then at the last minute speeds up and passes through the roadblock without stopping. According to the Guidelines

a. the officers should note the car's license number and radio headquarters
b. the officers should request back-up to pursue the car
c. the officer in the command observation vehicle should pursue the motorist
d. the officers conducting field sobriety tests should go to their cars pursue the vehicle

156. Based on the Guidelines, which of the following statements is true?

a. Guidelines for drunk-driving roadblocks are determined by the State Police.
b. Guidelines for drunk-driving roadblocks are determined by local police departments.
c. Guidelines for drunk-driving roadblocks are determined by the State Legislature.
d. Guidelines for drunk-driving roadblocks are determined by the County Sheriff.

157. According to the Guidelines, officers operating a drunk-driving roadblock can expect:

a. cooperation from most drivers
b. to arrest only about one percent of the drivers stopped
c. to issue several tickets for failure to wear a seat belt
d. that many cars will refuse to stop

158. According to the Guidelines, the main role of the command observation officer at a drunk-driving roadblock is to

a. conduct field sobriety tests
b. establish the official police presence
c. determine when to dismantle the roadblock
d. coordinate the roadblock

SET 22 (Answers begin on page 157.)

Here is more firefighter-related material. For the first series of questions, practice reading this simple table.

Compartment 1	Compartment 2
Ax	Nozzle
Pry bar	Two lengths of hose
Sledge hammer	Pipe wrench
Torch	Toolbox
Compartment 3	**Compartment 4**
Fire extinguishers	First aid kit
Fire fighting foam	Oxygen cylinder
Portable pump	Rescue rope

159. A firefighter's superior officer calls for more hose. In which compartment would the firefighter find it?

a. Compartment 1
b. Compartment 2
c. Compartment 3
d. Compartment 4

160. A firefighter is directed to bring a fire extinguisher and an ax to the rear of a fire building. Which compartment or compartments would the firefighter need to open?

a. Compartment 1
b. Compartments 2 and 3
c. Compartments 1 and 3
d. Compartment 3

161. At the scene of an accident, a firefighter needs the following: a tool box, a pry bar, and a first aid kit. The firefighter would find these items in

a. Compartments 1 and 2
b. Compartments 2, 3, and 4
c. Compartments 3 and 4
d. Compartments 1, 2, and 4

The rescue rope is an important tool in the fire department. It must be maintained in top condition and ready for the members' use at all times. The rope is inspected weekly, then rewound so it will be ready for immediate use. A rescue rope may be placed out service for the following reasons:

1. The rope has been used to carry the weight of two people during a rescue.
2. The strands have become frayed.
3. The rope has abrasions.
4. The rope has been exposed to extreme heat.
5. There are persistent rust stains on the rope.
6. The rope has been frozen during operations.
7. The rope has been exposed to acid or acid-containing substances.

162. Which of the following organizational scheme does the above list of instructions follow?
a. chronological order
b. hierarchical order
c. order of importance
d. order by topic

163. Which of the following is NOT listed as a reason to place the rescue rope out of service?
a. The rope is abraded.
b. The rope is more than five years old.
c. One end of the rope is frayed.
d. The rope has been exposed to extreme heat.

164. Firefighters use the rope to rescue a 105-pound woman and an infant. After the rescue, the rope should be
a. rewound for the next use
b. inspected at the fire station
c. placed out of service
d. left to burn at the fire scene

165. During inspection of the rescue rope, you notice a rust stain. With a brush and soapy water you clean the stain off. After this, the rope should be:
a. placed out of service
b. replaced with a new rope
c. rewound for further use
d. re-inspected by another firefighter

SET 23 (Answers begin on page 157.)

Whether you're on the job or in another type of situation altogether, you will probably, at some time, be asked to extract information from graphs or tables. Reading them takes skill, but they are effective and economical ways to get information across.

THE FUJITA–PEARSON TORNADO INTENSITY SCALE

Classification	Wind Speed	Damage
F0	72 MPH	Mild
F1	73–112 MPH	Moderate
F2	113–157 MPH	Significant
F3	158–206 MPH	Severe
F4	207–260 MPH	Devastating
F5	260–319 MPH	Cataclysmic
F6	319–379 MPH	Overwhelming

166. A tornado with a wind speed of 173 mph would be assigned which classification?
a. F0
b. F1
c. F2
d. F3

167. The names of the categories in the third column, labeled "Damage," could best be described as
a. scientific
b. descriptive
c. objective
d. whimsical

SET 24 (Answers begin on page 157.)

Tables like this one are a good way to present a lot of information in a way that's easy to understand. The ability to comprehend information presented this way is vital in today's "information age." Start by noticing the title of the table (in the black band) and the column headings (in boldface).

FOREST FIRES, TRI-COUNTY REGION
JUNE 1994

Date	Area	# of Acres Burned	Probable Cause
June 2	Burgaw Grove	115	Lightning
June 3	Fenner Forest	200	Campfire
June 7	Voorhees Air Base Training Site	400	Equipment Use
June 12	Murphy County Nature Reserve	495	Children
June 13	Knoblock Mountain	200	Misc.
June 14	Cougar Run Ski Center	160	Unknown
June 17	Fenner Forest	120	Campfire
June 19	Stone River State Park	526	Arson
June 21	Burgaw Grove	499	Smoking
June 25	Bramley Acres Resort	1,200	Arson
June 28	Hanesboro Crossing	320	Lightning
June 30	Stone River State Park	167	Campfire

168. According to the table, suspected arson fires
a. occurred at Stone River State Park and Hanesboro Crossing
b. consumed over 1,700 acres
c. occurred less frequently than fires caused by smoking
d. consumed fewer acres than fires caused by lightning

169. One week after the Voorhees Air Base fire, where did a fire occur?
a. Knoblock Mountain
b. Fenner Forest
c. Cougar Run Ski Center
d. Burgaw Grove

170. Which of the following incidents most likely started the Bramley Acres Resort fire?
a. After drinking to the point of intoxication, a group of teenagers passed out, leaving their picnic fire unattended.
b. A violent thunderstorm descended on the forest.
c. A lone deer hunter, angry at her husband, tossed a match into the tent where he was sleeping.
d. A man with no camping experience filled his camp-stove with gasoline, and it exploded.

SET 25 (Answers begin on page 158.)

Here are two tables such as you might be asked to read in a textbook or on the job. Note their simplicity and economy. With a little practice, you can master the art of reading tables quickly. Be sure to read the title and footnotes, if any, with care.

HURST COUNTY TOWNS, NUMBER OF DAYS WITHOUT SIGNIFICANT PRECIPITATION*

Town	# of Days	Status**
Riderville	38	level two
Adams	25	level one
Parkston	74	level three
Kings Hill	28	level two
West Granville	50	level three
Braxton	23	level three
Chase Crossing	53	level four
Livingston Center	45	level three

* *At least half an inch in a 48-hour period.*
** *The higher the level, the greater potential for fire.*

171. The status of the town with the LEAST number of days without significant precipitation is
a. level one
b. level two
c. level three
d. level four

172. Compared to Riderville, Livingston Center
a. is more likely to experience a fire
b. is less likely to experience a fire
c. is just as likely to experience a fire
d. has gone a shorter period without significant precipitation

DISTRIBUTION OF OCCUPATIONS OF 200 ADULT MALES IN THE BAIDYA CASTE, MADARIPUR VILLAGE, BENGAL, 1914

Occupation	Number
farmers	02
government service, clerks	44
lawyers	06
newspapers and presses	05
no occupation	25
not recorded	08
students	68
teachers	11
trade and commerce	23

173. The largest number of men in the Baidya caste of Madaripur are involved in which field?
a. education
b. agriculture
c. government
d. publishing

174. The smallest number of men in the Baidya caste of Madaripur are involved in which field?
a. education
b. agriculture
c. government
d. publishing

SET 26 (Answers begin on page 158.)

Here are job-related passages that are in text, rather than list or table, form, so it's a bit more difficult to discern the structure. Don't forget that marking up the passage or taking notes can help you simplify, absorb, and remember the information. Pick out the important points and number them, so they won't be lost in the blocks of text. As you number the points, look for the overall structure.

Often in the course of routine patrol, a police officer needs to briefly detain a person for questioning without an arrest warrant or even probable cause. The officer may also feel that it is necessary to frisk this person for weapons. This type of detention is known as a "Terry Stop," after the U.S. Supreme Court case Terry versus State of Ohio. In that case, the Court determined that a Terry Stop does not violate a citizen's right to be free from unreasonable search and seizure, as long as certain procedures are followed. First, the person must be behaving in some manner that arouses the police officer's suspicion. Second, the officer must believe that swift action is necessary to prevent a crime from being committed or a suspect from escaping. Finally, in order to frisk the individual, the officer must reasonably believe that the person is armed and dangerous. We will now look at each of these elements in more detail.

In determining whether an individual is acting in a suspicious manner, a police officer must rely on his or her training and experience. Circumstances in each case will be different, but an officer must be able to articulate what it was about a person's behavior that aroused suspicion, whether one particular action or a series of actions taken together. For example, it may not be unusual for shoppers in a store to wander up and down the aisles looking at merchandise. However, it may be suspicious if a person does this for an inordinate period of time, seems to be checking the locations of surveillance equipment, and is wearing loose clothing that would facilitate shoplifting. Similarly, it is not unusual for a person wearing gym shorts and a tee-shirt to be running through a residential neighborhood; however, a person dressed in regular clothes might legitimately be suspect. It is important to note that a person who simply appears out of place based, for example, on the manner in which he or she is dressed, is not alone cause for suspicion on the part of a police officer.

In addition to the behavior that arouses an officer's attention, the officer must believe that immediate action must be taken to prevent the commission of a crime or a suspect from escaping. In some situations, it may be better to wait to develop probable cause and arrest the person. One important element of this decision is the safety of any other people in the area. In addition, a police officer may determine that her or his immediate action is necessary to avert the commission of a crime, even if no people are in danger. If the suspect appears, for example, to be checking out parked cars for the possibility of stealing one, an officer may well be able to wait until the crime is in progress (thereby having probable cause for an arrest) or even until the crime is actually committed, when patrol cars can be dispatched to arrest the individual. On the other hand, a person who appears to be planning a carjacking should be stopped before the occupants of a car can be hurt. Again, an officer must make a quick decision based on all the circumstances.

Once an officer has detained a suspicious person, the officer must determine if he or she feels it is necessary to frisk the individual for weapons. Again, an officer should rely on her or his training and experience. If the officer feels that the detainee poses a threat to the officer's safety, the suspect should be frisked. For example, although there may certainly be exceptions, a person suspected of shoplifting is not likely to be armed. On the other hand, a person suspected of breaking and entering may very well be carrying a weapon. In addition, the officer should be aware of the behavior of the person once the stop is made. Certain behavior indicates the person is waiting for an opportunity to produce a weapon and threaten the officer's safety. The safety of the officer and any civilians in the area is the most important consideration.

175. Which of the following organizational schemes is most prevalent in the passage?
   a. comparison-contrast
   b. hierarchical order
   c. cause-and-effect
   d. chronological order

176. According to the reading passage, a "Terry Stop" is
   a. an arrest for shoplifting.
   b. the brief detention and questioning of a suspicious person.
   c. an officer's frisking a suspect for weapons.
   d. the development of a case that results in an arrest warrant.

177. According to the passage, a Terry Stop includes frisking a suspect if
   a. the officer sees evidence of a weapon
   b. the person is suspected of breaking and entering
   c. there are civilians in the area
   d. the officer or others are in danger

178. An officer on foot patrol notices two people standing on a street corner. The officer observes the two and, after a moment, one of the people walks slowly down the street, looks in the window of a store called McFadden's, walks on a few feet, then turns around and returns to the other person. They speak briefly, then the other person walks down the street, performing the same series of motions. They repeat this ritual five or six times each. The officer would be justified in performing a Terry Stop, based on her suspicion that the people
   a. appeared to be carrying weapons
   b. looked out of place
   c. might be planning to rob McFadden's
   d. were obstructing the sidewalk

179. According to the passage, an officer may choose to conduct a Terry Stop
   a. to discourage loitering
   b. to prevent a crime from being committed or a suspect from escaping
   c. to find out if a person is carrying a concealed weapon
   d. to rule out suspects after a crime has been committed

180. According to the passage, the determination that a person is suspicious
   a. depends on the circumstances of each situation.
   b. means someone looks out of place.
   c. usually means someone is guilty of planning a crime.
   d. usually indicates a person is carrying a concealed weapon.

181. An officer has stopped a suspicious individual. The suspect seems to be trying to reach for something under her coat. The officer should
a. call for back-up.
b. arrest the suspect.
c. frisk the suspect.
d. handcuff the suspect.

182. An officer observes a person sitting on a bench outside a bank at 4:30 p.m. The officer knows the bank closes at 5:00. The person checks his watch several times and watches customers come and go through the door of the bank. He also makes eye contact with a person driving a blue sedan, that appears to be circling the block. Finally, a parking space in front of the bank becomes vacant and the sedan pulls in. The driver and the man on the bench nod to each other. The officer believes the two are planning to rob the bank right before it closes. The officer should
a. immediately begin questioning the man on the bench, since it appears he's going to rob the bank.
b. immediately begin questioning the driver of the sedan, since it appears she's driving the getaway car.
c. go into the bank, warn the employees, and ask all the customers to leave for their own safety.
d. call for back-up, since it appears the potential robbers are waiting for the bank to close.

183. According to the United States Supreme Court, a Terry Stop
a. is permissible search and seizure
b. often occurs in the course of police work
c. should only be undertaken when two officers are present
d. requires probable cause

184. According to the passage, persons suspected of shoplifting
a. should never be frisked as shoplifters rarely carry weapons
b. may legitimately be the subjects of a Terry Stop
c. always wear loose clothing and wander in the store a long time
d. may be handcuffed immediately for the safety of the civilians in the area

185. An officer in a squad car is patrolling a wealthy residential neighborhood. She notices one house in which a light will come on in one part of the house for a few minutes, then go off. A moment later, a light will come on in another part of the house, then go off. This happens several times in different parts of the house. The officer also notes that the garage door is standing open and there are no cars parked there or in the driveway. The officer believes there may be a burglary in progress and pulls over to observe the house. While she is watching the house, a man wearing torn jeans and a dirty tee shirt walks by the house, pauses to fix his shoelace, then walks on. According to the passage, the officer should not
a. allow the man to see her as he may be dangerous
b. involve the neighbors by asking them if they have information.
c. stop the man as there is no indication he is involved in criminal activity.
d. radio headquarters until she is absolutely sure a crime is being committed

SET 27 (Answers begin on page 158.)

Here is another set of job-related instructions presented in text, rather than list form. Keep in mind what you practiced earlier. Don't forget that a good reader is an active reader. Look at the organization of the passage. Take notes. Try making an outline.

Due to recent national events, the Yardley City Government has introduced new bomb threat procedures for government buildings. This information is for department use only.

From this point on, all personnel must be on the highest alert. You must pay close attention to your surroundings. If a vehicle you do not recognize enters the parking lot, observe driver and passenger behavior. If an employee has been terminated recently, examine his or her performance evaluations and exit interview reports. If there are incidents involving visitors, notify your supervisor. Keep in mind, however, that we must not overreact. Part of being alert is exercising proper judgment.

If there is an actual bomb threat, carry out the following procedures: First, evacuate the premises. Do not fall into fire drill routines; remember, you are vacating in order to avoid injury stemming from premeditated violence. Leave the building immediately. Take nothing with you. Do not shut down electrical equipment. Keep movement to a minimum. If there are visitors and/or persons with special needs in the building, make certain they are evacuated.

Proceed to the area AWAY from the building designated in the fire drill policy. Do not enter vehicles parked nearby. Take attendance. Make mental notes about any missing personnel or any questionable activity in or near the building. If you received the actual threat, record as much information as possible: gender, specific language, "insider" information, type of violence threatened. Once you reach your designated safe area, identify emergency personnel and share the information with them.

186. Which of the following organizational scheme does the passage mainly follow?
a. hierarchical order
b. chronological order
c. order by topic
d. cause-and-effect

187. The passage as a whole suggests that, during an actual bomb threat incident, the most important priority is to
a. avoid overreacting
b. follow proper procedures
c. notify the supervisor of suspicious activities
d. keep the bomb threat information inside the department

188. Which of the following is NOT included in this passage?
a. where to go in the event of a bomb threat
b. what to do if an unknown vehicle parks near the station
c. what to do with specific bomb threat information
d. how to identify a potentially dangerous fired employee

189. If there is a bomb threat incident, and you have previously seen a visitor enter the building in a wheelchair, you should
a. direct the visitor to the designated evacuation area
b. notify your supervisor
c. notify emergency personnel
d. carefully observe the visitor's behavior

Firefighters are often called upon to speak to school and community groups about the importance of fire safety, particularly fire prevention and detection. Because smoke detectors cut in half a person's risk of dying in a fire, firefighters often provide audiences with information on how to install these protective devices in their homes.

A smoke detector should be placed on each floor level of a home. Because sleeping persons are in particular danger if a fire starts, there must be one outside each sleeping area. A good site for a detector would be a hallway that runs between living spaces and bedrooms.

Because of the "dead" air space that might be missed by turbulent hot air bouncing around above a fire, smoke detectors should be installed either on the ceiling at least four inches from the nearest wall, or high on a wall at least four but no further than twelve inches from the ceiling.

Detectors should not be mounted near windows, exterior doors, or other places where drafts might direct the smoke away from the unit. Nor should they be placed in kitchens and garages, where cooking and gas fumes are likely to set off false alarms.

190. Which of the following organizational schemes does the above list of instructions make most use of?
a. hierarchical order
b. comparison-contrast
c. cause-and-effect
d. chronological order

191. What is the main focus of this passage?
a. how firefighters carry out their responsibilities
b. the proper installation of home smoke detectors
c. the detection of "dead" air space on walls and ceilings
d. how smoke detectors prevent fires in homes

192. The passage implies that "dead" air space is most likely to be found
a. on a ceiling, between four and twelve inches from a wall
b. close to where a wall meets a ceiling
c. near an open window
d. in kitchens and garages

193. The passage states that, when compared with people who do not have smoke detectors, persons who live in homes with smoke detectors have a
a. 50% better chance of surviving a fire
b. 50% better chance of preventing a fire
c. 75% better chance of detecting a hidden fire
d. 100% better chance of not being injured in a fire

194. A smoke detector should NOT be installed near a window because
a. outside fumes may trigger a false alarm
b. a wind draft may create a "dead" air space
c. a wind draft may pull smoke away from the detector
d. outside noises may muffle the sound of the detector

195. The passage indicates that one responsibility of a firefighter is to
  a. install smoke detectors in the homes of residents in the community
  b. check homes to see if smoke detectors have been properly installed
  c. develop fire safety programs for community leaders and school teachers to use
  d. speak to school children about the importance of preventing fires

196. A smoke detector must always be placed
  a. outside at least one of the bedrooms on any level of the home
  b. outside all bedrooms in a home
  c. in all hallways of a home
  d. in kitchens where fires are most likely to start

SET 28 (Answers begin on page 159.)

Many times more than one organizational scheme is used in a single block of text, although there is usually one that predominates.

Firefighters must learn the proper procedures for responding to residential carbon monoxide (CO) emergencies.

Upon arriving at the scene of the alarm, personnel shall put on protective clothing and then bring an operational, calibrated CO meter onto the premises.

Occupants of the premises shall then be examined. If they are experiencing CO poisoning symptoms—i.e., headaches, nausea, confusion, dizziness, and other flu-like symptoms—an emergency medical services (EMS) crew shall be notified immediately and the occupants evacuated and administered oxygen.

To test for CO contamination, meters must be held head high. Appliances should be operating for five to ten minutes before testing, and a check must be made near all gas appliances and vents. If vents are working properly, no CO emissions will enter the structure.

If the meters register unsafe levels—above 10 parts per million (ppm)—all occupants shall be evacuated and the source of the contamination investigated. Occupants shall be interviewed to ascertain the location of the CO detector (if any), the length of time the alarm has sounded, what the occupants were doing at the time of the alarm (cooking, etc.), and what electrical appliances were functioning. Occupants shall not re-enter the premises until the environment is deemed safe.

If the meters register levels lower than nine ppm, occupants shall be allowed to re-enter the building. They shall be notified of the recorded level and given a CO informational packet.

197. Which two main organizational schemes can be identified in the above list of instructions?
a. hierarchical order and order by topic
b. order by topic and comparison-contrast
c. hierarchical order and chronological order
d. chronological order and cause-and-effect

198. If residents are experiencing carbon monoxide poisoning symptoms, which of the following steps should firefighters take immediately?
a. allow the residents to lie down
b. determine CO levels in the household
c. summon an emergency services team
d. investigate the source of contamination

199. Carbon monoxide levels under nine ppm are considered
a. relatively safe
b. very dangerous
c. capable of causing illness
d. cause for evacuation

200. According to the passage, all occupants of a residence should be evacuated when
a. the investigators arrive
b. an EMS crew arrives
c. the source of contamination is discovered
d. any occupant exhibits symptoms of CO poisoning

201. Which of the following is NOT included in this passage?
a. potential sources of contamination
b. indications of CO toxicity
c. proper levels of oxygen for ailing occupants
d. which pieces of equipment should be taken into homes

SET 29 (Answers begin on page 159.)

This set contains two relatively straightforward lists of job-related tasks. Put to use what you've learned so far. Underline or make notes on important points. Look at structure. Don't forget to look for the main idea of the passage. Consider the purpose for which the passage was written.

Preserving evidence is not your main priority as a firefighter, yet certain steps can be taken, while fighting a fire, to maintain site integrity and maximize the efforts of investigators.

First, try to determine the point of origin from wind direction or the way the fire spread.

If you suspect arson or human error, you should take notes, mentally and on paper, of concrete evidence. Look for suspicious people or vehicles. Use ribbon or other practical material to flag potential evidence, such as tracks near the suspected point of origin and items such as matches, bottles, rags, cigarette butts, lighters, paper, or exposed wires. Keep other personnel away from these areas unless doing so would hamper fire fighting efforts.

After flagging the evidence, notify the commanding officer as soon as possible. If evidence must be removed, handle it carefully to maintain fingerprint integrity.

Once the fire is declared under control, create a map of the scene, indicating the point of origin and areas where evidence is or was located. Compose an inventory of any evidence that was removed. Record any other useful information, such as conversations with witnesses, names, and descriptions. Before leaving, share your findings with the lead investigator.

Remember, safety is the main priority during fighting of the fire. But by keeping an alert eye for clues, you can also contribute to an efficient investigation into its cause.

202. Which of the following organizational patterns is the main one used in the passage?

a. chronological order
b. hierarchical order
c. comparison-contrast
d. cause-and-effect

203. According to the passage, which of the following is the main responsibility of a firefighter?

a. to maintain the integrity of the site
b. to flag evidence and keep an inventory of it
c. to operate in a safe manner
d. to provide support for investigators

204. The passage suggests that the first step the firefighter should take after evidence is flagged is to

a. bring it to the attention of the officer in command
b. create a map of the scene
c. see how it relates to the point of origin
d. indicate its location to investigators

205. Which of the following would a firefighter NOT necessarily do after the fire is brought under control?

a. create an inventory
b. carefully remove the evidence from the scene
c. log witness descriptions
d. record flagged evidence areas

206. Which of the following best expresses the subject of this passage?

a. how to aid investigation into the cause of a fire
b. how to maintain safety while investigating a fire
c. the importance of flagging evidence during the fighting of a fire
d. what to do with flagged evidence of the cause of a fire

207. According to the passage, fire personnel should be instructed to avoid areas where evidence is found

a. only after the fire has been brought under control
b. only if the fire can also be fought effectively
c. only if the evidence points directly to the cause of the fire
d. only until the commanding officer is informed

In October of 1993, a disastrous wildfire swept across portions of Charlesburg. Five residents were killed, 320 homes destroyed, and 19,500 acres burned. A public safety task force was formed to review emergency response. The task force findings were as follows:

- The water supply in the residential areas was insufficient, and some hydrants could not even be opened. The task force recommended a review of hydrant inspection policy.
- Fire companies that responded had difficulty locating specific sites. Most came from other areas and were not familiar with Charlesburg. The available maps were outdated and did not reflect recent housing developments.
- Evacuation procedures were inadequate. Residents reported being given conflicting and/or confusing information. Some residents of the Hilltop Estates subdivision ignored mandatory evacuation orders, yet others were praised for their cooperation.
- Firefighters reported a number of items that contributed to the spread of the fires. Some homes were lost long after the fire had passed through, because dried undergrowth nearby caught fire and slowly spread.
- Homeowners had not been sufficiently educated on emergency preparedness. Many residents underestimated hazards such as shifting winds, poor visibility due to smoke, and the speed with which fire spreads.

208. Which of the following organizational patterns is the main one used in the passage?
a. chronological order
b. hierarchical order
c. order by topic
d. cause-and-effect

209. According to the passage, why did some fire companies have difficulty adequately responding to the Charlesburg fire?
a. Visibility was poor, due to smoke.
b. They were given conflicting information.
c. They lacked knowledge about Charlesburg streets.
d. They could not locate water sources.

210. According to the passage, which of the following was a specific task force recommendation?
a. Evacuation shelters should be better supplied.
b. Residents of Hilltop Estates should be reprimanded.
c. Outdated maps should be destroyed.
d. Hydrant inspection procedures should be reexamined.

211. One reason for confusion among some homeowners was that
a. they lacked adequate guidance on emergency procedures
b. their subdivisions were not included on emergency maps
c. they could not locate emergency shelters
d. they misunderstood hydrant inspection policy

212. Which of the following is NOT included in this passage?
a. the reason some homes burned after the main fire had swept through
b. statistics based on the aftermath of the fire
c. the role played by wind direction
d. the home cities of other fire departments who responded

SET 30 (Answers begin on page 160.)

Here are two more straightforward, job-related passages. Again, pay special attention to organization. Try a simple outline of the passages to aid comprehension.

As a firefighter, you may be assigned the important task of conducting school fire inspections. At the school, you should first meet with school officials to discuss fire safety policy. Be certain all those involved, including administrators, teachers, and support staff, understand their roles during emergencies. Ask about the school's fire drill schedule and inquire about your department's participation in future drills.

Next, conduct a check of all alarms on the premises. If an alarm has been tampered with, notify school officials immediately. If an alarm is not functioning properly and cannot be repaired immediately, notify school officials and fill out a repair request form.

Next, inspect all exits to be sure none are obstructed. Review evacuation plans to make certain primary and secondary exits are viable. Walk the routes yourself.

Next, inspect all extinguishers. Remember, pressurized water extinguishers must NOT be located near electrical equipment. If this is the case, they should be replaced immediately with foam units, which are safer.

Finally, inspect wall and ceiling decorations. Depending on regulations, it is often a violation of fire codes to have more than 20 percent of any wall or ceiling covered with artwork or other hangings. Last, report your findings to your supervisor.

213. Which of the following organizational patterns is the main one used in the passage?

a. chronological order
b. hierarchical order
c. comparison-contrast
d. cause-and-effect

214. According the passage, why should fire personnel review evacuation plans?

a. to confirm that all exits listed are workable options
b. to inspect the alarms located near exits
c. to replace pressurized water extinguishers
d. to notify school officials if alarms are malfunctioning

215. Why should pressurized water extinguishers located near electrical equipment be replaced?

a. They cannot be easily repaired.
b. They obstruct emergency exits.
c. Their use requires extensive training.
d. They are a potential threat to safety.

216. Which of the following is NOT included in this passage?

a. what to do if an alarm is damaged
b. a review of staff responsibility during an emergency
c. the procedure to follow if an exit is blocked
d. the significance of material attached to ceilings

217. Which of the following safety measures is covered in the passage?

a. how to correctly perform a fire drill
b. how to tell if an alarm has been tampered with
c. how to identify a particularly hazardous wall or ceiling hanging
d. how to tell if a certain pressurized water extinguisher should be replaced

If a building is to be left in a safe condition, firefighters must search for hidden fires that may rekindle. Typically, this process, known as overhaul, begins in the area of actual fire involvement. Before searching for hidden fires, however, firefighters must first determine the condition of the building.

The fire's intensity and the amount of water used to fight the fire are both factors that affect a building. Fire can burn away floor joists and weaken roof trusses. Heat from the fire can weaken concrete and the mortar in wall joints and elongate steel roof supports. Excess water can add dangerous weight to floors and walls.

Once it has been determined that it is safe to enter a building, the process of overhauling begins. A firefighter can often detect hidden fires by looking for discolorations, peeling paint, cracked plaster, and smoke emissions; by feeling walls and floors with the back of the hand; by listening for popping, cracking, and hissing sounds; and by using electronic sensors to detect heat variances.

218. Which of the following sentences from the passage is an example of explicitly stated cause-and-effect?

a. "Typically, this process, known as overhaul, begins in the area of actual fire involvement."
b. "Before searching for hidden fires, however, firefighters must first determine the condition of the building."
c. "Once it has been determined that it is safe to enter a building, the process of overhauling begins."
d. "A firefighter can often detect hidden fires by looking for discolorations, peeling paint, cracked plaster, and smoke emissions. . . ."

219. The main purpose of overhauling a building is to

a. strengthen wall joints and roof supports
b. make sure the fire will not start up again
c. make sure excess water has not damaged floors
d. test for heat damage by using electronic sensors

220. Before overhauling a building, what is the *first* thing a firefighter should do?

a. Look for discolorations in the paint
b. Detect differences in heat along walls and floors
c. Listen for sounds that may indicate a fire
d. Determine the extent of fire and water damage

221. According to the passage, cracked plaster is a sign that

a. a wall may be about to fall in
b. a fire may be smoldering inside a wall
c. a wall is dangerously weighted with water
d. firefighters should exit the building immediately

SET 31 (Answers begin on page 160.)

Outlining a reading passage can help you discern its overall meaning. The next three sets present passages such as you might find in textbooks. Each contains one question that asks you to identify an outline that might fit the passage. In these sets you will also begin to draw more complex inferences—that is, to identify ideas that are not explicitly stated in the passages.

(1) The coast of the State of Maine is one of the most irregular in the world. A straight line running from the southernmost city in Maine, Kittery, to the northernmost coastal city, Eastport, would measure about 225 miles. If you followed the coastline between the same two cities, you would travel more than ten times as far. This irregularity is the result of what is called a *drowned coastline.* The term comes from the glacial activity of the ice age. At that time, the whole area that is now Maine was part of a mountain range that towered above the sea. As the glacier descended, however, it expended enormous force on those mountains and they sank into the sea.

(2) As the mountains sank, ocean water charged over the lowest parts of the remaining land, forming a series of twisting inlets and lagoons, of contorted grottos and nooks. Once the glacier receded, the highest parts of the former mountain range that were nearest the shore remained as islands. Although the mountain ranges were never to return, the land rose somewhat over the centuries. On Mt. Desert Island, one of the most famous of the islands the glacier left behind in its retreat from the coast of Maine, marine fossils have been found at 225 feet above today's sea level, indicating that level was once the shoreline.

(3) The 2500-mile-long rocky and jagged coastline of Maine keeps watch over nearly two thousand islands. Many of these islands are tiny and uninhabited, but many are home to thriving communities. Mt. Desert Island is one of the largest—sixteen miles long and nearly twelve miles wide—and one of the most beautiful of the Maine coast islands. Mt. Desert very nearly formed as two distinct islands. It is split almost in half by Somes Sound, a very deep and very narrow stretch of water seven miles long. On the east side of the island, Cadillac Mountain rises fifteen hundred and thirty two feet, making it the highest mountain on the Atlantic seaboard.

(4) For years, Mt. Desert Island, particularly its major settlement, Bar Harbor, afforded summer homes for the wealthy. Recently, Bar Harbor has made a name for itself as a burgeoning arts community as well. But there is much more to Mt. Desert Island than a sophisticated and wealthy playground. A majority of the island is unspoiled forest land, and it makes up the greatest part of Acadia National Park. Mt. Desert Island sits on the boundary line between the temperate and sub-Arctic zones. The island, therefore, supports the flora and fauna of both zones, as well as beach, inland, and alpine plants. And, Mt. Desert Island lies in a major bird migration lane; all kinds of migratory birds pass over the island. All this is in addition to its geological treasures.

(5) The establishment of Acadia National Park in 1916 means that this diversity of nature will be preserved and that it will be available to all people, not just the wealthy who once had exclusive access to the island's natural beauty. Today, visitors to Acadia may receive nature instruction from the park naturalists, in addition to enjoying the beauty of the island by camping, hiking, cycling, or boating. Or visitors may choose to spend time at the archeological museum, learning about the Stone Age inhabitants of the island. The best view on Mt. Desert Island, though, is from the top of Cadillac Mountain. From the summit, you can gaze back toward the mainland or out over the Atlantic Ocean and contemplate the beauty created by a retreating glacier.

222. Which of the following lists of topics best outlines the information in the selection?

a. — Ice-age glacial activity
   — The Islands of Casco Bay
   — Formation of Cadillac Mountain
   — Summer residents of Mt. Desert Island

b. — Formation of a drowned coastline
   — The topography of Mt. Desert Island
   — The environment of Mt. Desert Island
   — Tourist attractions on Mt. Desert Island

c. — Mapping the Maine coastline
   — The arts community at Bar Harbor
   — History of the National Park system
   — Climbing Cadillac Mountain

d. — The effect of glaciers on small islands
   — Stone-age dwellers on Mt. Desert Island
   — The importance of bio-diversity
   — Hiking in Acadia National Park

223. Which of the following statements best expresses the main idea of paragraph four of the selection?

a. The wealthy residents of Mt. Desert Island selfishly kept it to themselves.
b. Acadia National Park is one of the smallest of the national parks.
c. On Mt. Desert Island, there is great tension between the year-round residents and the summer tourists.
d. Due to its location and environment, Mt. Desert Island supports an incredibly diverse animal and plant life.

224. According to the selection, the large number of small islands along the coast of Maine are the result of

a. glaciers forcing a mountain range into the sea
b. Maine's location between the temperate and sub-Arctic zones
c. the irregularity of the Maine coast
d. the need for summer communities for wealthy tourists and artists

225. The content of paragraph five indicates that the writer believes that

a. the continued existence of national parks is threatened by budget cuts
b. the best way to preserve the environment on Mt. Desert Island is to limit the number of visitors
c. national parks allow large numbers of people to visit and learn about interesting wilderness areas
d. Mt. Desert Island is the most interesting tourist attraction in Maine

226. According to the selection, the coast of Maine is

a. 2500 miles long
b. 3500 miles long
c. 225 miles long
d. 235 miles long

SET 32 (Answers begin on page 160.)

Here is another passage such as you might find in a textbook. Again, remember that outlining is one approach to good reading comprehension. When you finish reading the passage, try outlining it and see how your outline compares with those in the question immediately following the passage.

Mental and physical health professionals may consider referring clients and patients to a music therapist for a number of reasons. It seems a particularly good choice for the social worker who is coordinating a client's case. Music therapists use music to establish a relationship with the patient and to improve the patient's health, using highly structured musical interactions. Patients and therapists may sing, play instruments, compose music, dance, or simply listen to music.

The course of training for music therapists is comprehensive. In addition to their formal musical and therapy training, music therapists are taught to discern what kinds of interventions will be most beneficial for each individual patient. Since each patient is different and has different goals, the music therapist must be able to understand the patient's situation and choose the music and activities that will do the most toward helping the patient achieve his or her goals. The referring social worker can help this process by clearly articulating each client's history.

Although patients may develop their musical skills, that is not the main goal of music therapy. Any client who needs particular work on communication or on academic, emotional, and social skills, and who is not responding to traditional therapy, is an excellent candidate for music therapy.

227. Which of the following best organizes the main topics addressed in this passage?

a. I. The role of music therapy in social work
   II. Locating a music therapist
   III. How to complete a music therapist referral

b. I. Using music in therapy
   II. A typical music therapy intervention
   III. When to prescribe music therapy for sociopaths

c. I. Music therapy and social work
   II. Training for music therapists
   III. Skills addressed by music therapy

d. I. How to choose a music therapist
   II. When to refer to a music therapist
   III. Who benefits the most from music therapy

228. Which of the following would be the most appropriate title for this passage?

a. How to Use Music to Combat Depression
b. Music Therapy: A Role in Social Work?
c. Training for a Career in Music Therapy
d. The Social Worker as Music Therapist

229. According to information presented in the passage, music therapy can be prescribed for social work clients who

a. need to develop coping skills
b. were orphaned as children
c. need to resolve family issues
d. need to improve social skills

230. Which of the following inferences can be drawn from the passage?

a. Music therapy can succeed where traditional therapies have failed.
b. Music therapy is a relatively new field.
c. Music therapy is particularly beneficial for young children.
d. Music therapy is only appropriate in a limited number of circumstances.

SET 33 (Answers begin on page 161.)

Here's a more difficult passage such as you might find quoted in a law textbook. It is from the landmark case *Brown v. Board of Education* (1954), which helped end segregation of American schools based on race.

(1) These cases come to us from the States of Kansas, South Carolina, Virginia, and Delaware. . . . Argument was heard in the 1952 Term and reargument was heard this Term on certain questions propounded by the Court.

(2) Reargument was largely devoted to the circumstances surrounding the adoption of the 14th Amendment in 1868. It covered exhaustively consideration of the Amendment in Congress, ratification by the states, then existing practices in racial segregation, and the views of proponents and opponents of the Amendment. These sources and our own investigation convince us that, although these sources cast some light, it is not enough to resolve the problem with which we are faced. At best, they are inconclusive. The most avid proponents of the post-War Amendments undoubtedly intended them to remove all legal distinctions among "all persons born or naturalized in the United States." Their opponents, just as certainly, were antagonistic to both the letter and the spirit of the Amendments and wished them to have the most limited effect. What others in Congress and the state legislatures had in mind cannot be determined with any degree of certainty.

(3) An additional reason for the inconclusive nature of the Amendment's history, with respect to segregated schools, is the status of public education at that time. In the South, the movement toward free common schools, supported by general taxation, had not yet taken hold. . . . Even in the North, the conditions of public education did not approximate those existing today. The curriculum was usually rudimentary; ungraded schools were common in rural areas; compulsory school attendance was virtually unknown. As a consequence, it is not surprising that there should be so little, in the history of the 14th Amendment relating to its intended effect on public education.

(4) In approaching this problem, we cannot turn the clock back to 1868, when the [14th] Amendment was adopted, . . . We must consider public education in the light of its full development and its present place in American life throughout the Nation. . . . Today, education is perhaps the most important function of state and local governments. Compulsory school attendance laws and the great expenditures for education both demonstrate our recognition of the importance of education to our democratic society. It is required in the performance of our most basic public responsibilities, even service in the armed forces. It is the very foundation of good citizenship. Today it is a principal instrument in awakening the child to cultural values, in preparing him for later professional training, and in helping him to adjust normally to his environment. In these days, it is doubtful that any child may reasonably be expected to succeed in life if he is denied the opportunity of an education. Such an opportunity, where the state has undertaken to provide it, is a right which must be made available to all on equal terms. . . .

(5) We conclude that in the field of public education . . . [s]eparate educational facilities are inherently unequal. Therefore, we hold that the plaintiffs and others similarly situated for whom the actions have been brought are . . . deprived of equal protection.

231. Which of the following organizational schemes figures most prominently in the passage?
   a. hierarchical order
   b. order by topic
   c. comparison-contrast
   d. chronological order

232. Which of the following sets of topics would best organize the information in the selection?

a. I. The Supreme Court's role in public education
   II. The role of state government in public education

b. I. The history of the 14th Amendment
   II. The cost of public education

c. I. The 14th Amendment and public education
   II. The importance of public education for individuals and the country

d. I. The role of Congress in funding public education
   II. The evolution of public education

233. The selection indicates that the *plaintiffs* referred to in paragraph five were

a. not represented by attorneys
b. public school students
c. school board members
d. public school teachers

234. In paragraph 2, the phrase *post-War Amendments* refers to

a. Constitutional amendments dealing with education
b. the Bill of Rights
c. Constitutional amendments dealing with the military
d. The 14th and other Constitutional amendments, adopted after the Civil War

235. Use of the term *reargument* in paragraphs 1 and 2 would indicate that

a. on occasion, the U.S. Supreme Court hears arguments on the same case more than once
b. the plaintiffs were not adequately prepared the first time they argued
c. one or more Justices was absent during the first argument
d. the membership of the Supreme Court changed after the first argument

236. According to paragraph 3 of the selection, the Court determined that it is not clear what impact Congress intended the 14th Amendment to have on public education because

a. Congress generally does not deal with public education
b. public education was not universally available nor standardized at the time
c. in 1868, no transcripts of Congressional debates were kept
d. the Court disagreed with Congress' intentions

SET 34 (Answers begin on page 161.)

When you're reading at home it's best to keep a dictionary close at hand to look up words you don't know. In some settings, however, you may not have a dictionary handy, and you'll have to depend on the context of the word to lead you to the meaning. Start with the vocabulary in these individual sentences. For the words that are unfamiliar, see if you can choose the answer without looking at a dictionary.

237. The Adamsville Kennel Club's computer system, having been installed fifteen years ago, was <u>outmoded</u>.

a. worthless
b. unusable
c. obsolete
d. unnecessary

238. Although Marty Albertson's after-hours security job was regarded by many as so <u>menial</u> as to be beneath him, he liked the peace and solitude it offered.

a. boring
b. unpleasant
c. lowly
d. unrewarding

239. The actor's malice toward his co-star was revealed in his <u>vindictive</u> remarks, which almost ruined her career.

a. spiteful
b. outrageous
c. insulting
d. offensive

240. Although Mr. Chen is too ill to live alone, he is a headstrong man and <u>obstinately</u> refuses to move into a nursing home.

a. repeatedly
b. reluctantly
c. foolishly
d. stubbornly

241. The student's <u>glib</u> remarks trivialized the subject and irritated the teacher.

a. angry
b. superficial
c. insulting
d. dishonest

242. For all the problems faced by his district, Congressman Owly regarded budget cuts as a the answer to every problem, a complete <u>panacea</u>.

a. cure
b. result
c. cause
d. necessity

243. On the witness stand, the suspect, usually a flashy dresser, appeared uncharacteristically nondescript.
a. lethargic
b. undistinguished
c. indisposed
d. impeccable

244. Most members of the impoverished community regarded the councilman's phony British accent as pompous and his expensive, showy car as ostentatious.
a. hilarious
b. pretentious
c. outrageous
d. obnoxious

245. You cannot join the team without the prerequisite three-hour course in volleyball.
a. required
b. optional
c. preferred
d. advisable

246. According to the code of conduct, "Every officer will be held accountable for his or her decisions."
a. applauded
b. compensated
c. responsible
d. approached

SET 35 (Answers begin on page 162.)

Here are more sentences. Again, it's best to do this exercise without a dictionary. Let the context of the word guide you to the definition.

247. The two sisters, excited by seeing one another after so many years, became involved in an animated conversation.
a. abbreviated
b. civil
c. secret
d. lively

248. In order to keep our customers' business, their complaints must be handled in a diplomatic manner.
a. tactful
b. delaying
c. elaborate
d. combative

249. The residents of that area, knowing that seat belts save lives, are compliant with the seat belt law.
a. skeptical
b. obedient
c. forgetful
d. appreciative

250. Following the disturbance, town officials felt the need to augment the laws pertaining to mass demonstrations.
a. repeal
b. evaluate
c. expand
d. criticize

251. Although the neighborhood was said to be safe, they were repeatedly awakened, bothered by intermittent gunfire all night long.
a. protracted
b. periodic
c. incredulous
d. vehement

252. As soon as the details of the affair were released to the media, the newspaper was inundated with calls—far too many to be handled effectively.
a. provided
b. bothered
c. rewarded
d. flooded

253. The Marion Police Department's policy of aggressively recruiting women officers is unmatched, unique in every way.
a. rigorous
b. admirable
c. unparalleled
d. remarkable

254. When people heard that timid Bob had taken up sky-diving, they were incredulous.
a. fearful
b. outraged
c. convinced
d. disbelieving

255. The police department enthusiastically hired Officer Long because she was proficient in the use of computers to track down deadbeats.
a. sincere
b. adequate
c. competent
d. skilled

256. Not wanting to commit itself wholeheartedly, the City Council gave tentative approval to the idea of banning smoking from all public buildings.
a. provisional
b. ambiguous
c. wholehearted
d. unnecessary

SET 36 (Answers begin on page 162.)

Again, for these exercises, try working without a dictionary.

257. Regarding the need for more free coffee and doughnuts, the group's opinion was enthusiastic and unanimous.
a. divided
b. uniform
c. adamant
d. spirited

258. Since the townspeople were so dissatisfied, various methods to alleviate the situation were debated.
a. ease
b. tolerate
c. clarify
d. intensify

259. The officer was an indispensable member of the department, so they had no choice but to offer him a higher salary to stay on.
a. determined
b. experienced
c. essential
d. creative

260. The attorney wanted to expedite the process, as her client was becoming impatient.
a. accelerate
b. evaluate
c. reverse
d. justify

261. The suspect gave a plausible explanation for his presence at the scene, so the police decided to look elsewhere for the perpetrator of the crime.
a. unbelievable
b. credible
c. insufficient
d. apologetic

262. He based his conclusion on what he inferred from the evidence, not on what he actually observed.
a. intuited
b. imagined
c. surmised
d. implied

263. The neighborhood watch group presented its ultimatum to the drug dealers: move out or get busted.
a. earnest plea
b. formal petition
c. solemn promise
d. non-negotiable demand

264. The county coroner was determined to find the cause of death, no matter how well-disguised it might be, so her examination of the body was meticulous.
a. delicate
b. painstaking
c. superficial
d. objective

265. The general public didn't care about the trial and so was apathetic about the verdict.
a. enraged
b. indifferent
c. suspicious
d. saddened

266. The psychologists were pleased that their theory had been fortified by the new research.
a. reinforced
b. altered
c. disputed
d. developed

SET 37 (Answers begin on page 162.)

Finding meaning through context is a good example of active reading.

267. The captain often delegated responsibility to his subordinates, so as to have time to do the important tasks himself.
a. analyzed
b. respected
c. criticized
d. assigned

268. The awful truth about toxic waste dumping in their neighborhood aroused many community members.
a. informed
b. appeased
c. provoked
d. deceived

269. The spokesperson must articulate the philosophy of an entire department so that outsiders can understand it completely.
a. trust
b. refine
c. verify
d. express

270. The new shipping and receiving building is an expansive facility, large enough to meet our growing needs.
a. obsolete
b. meager
c. spacious
d. costly

271. The attorneys were now certain they could not win the case, since the ruling had proved to be so detrimental to their argument.
a. decisive
b. harmful
c. worthless
d. advantageous

272. My brother drives us crazy by crooning in the shower.
a. hooting
b. warbling
c. crying
d. shouting

273. The emotional fallout from a sexual assault can adversely affect one's later life, affecting the victim for years.
a. conflict
b. issues
c. relationship
d. consequences

274. The rain forest air was humid, making the heat seem even more smothering than before.
a. hot
b. damp
c. hazy
d. volitile

275. The balloon, loose from its string, rose up into the sky, a shiny purple sphere.
a. circle
b. globe
c. ovoid
d. nodule

SET 38 (Answers begin on page 163.)

Remember that the same word may have different meanings depending on the context.

276. After the storm caused raw sewage to seep into the ground water, the Water Department had to take measures to decontaminate the city's water supply.
a. refine
b. revive
c. freshen
d. purify

277. The mayor tailored his speech to suit the crowd of homeless people gathered in his office.
a. intoned
b. expanded
c. altered
d. shortened

278. The volcano lay dormant now, but we felt sure it would erupt again within the year.
a. inactive
b. slack
c. elevated
d. inattentive

279. Because of his disregard for his father's laws, the prince was punished by being banished from the kingdom.
a. apart
b. kidnapped
c. exiled
d. spirited

280. I relinquished my place in line to go back and talk with my friend Myrtle.
a. defended
b. yielded
c. delayed
d. remanded

281. I wrote in my journal every day, hoping in the future to author a book about my trip to Paris.
a. notebook
b. chapbook
c. diary
d. ledger

282. The thief jostled me in a crowd and was thus able to pick my pocket.
a. mugged
b. bumped
c. assailed
d. hindered

283. While we traveled in Italy we stayed in a hostel.
a. inn
b. compound
c. home
d. four-star hotel

284. My friend asked me to lie for her, but it's against my philosophy.
a. principles
b. regulations
c. personality
d. introspection

SET 39 (Answers begin on page 163.)

The first three questions in this set ask you to fill in the blank. Then you'll be asked to identify words in the context of a paragraph rather than in a single sentence. Remember, like a good detective, look at the context for clues to the meaning. Read closely.

285. When I bought my fancy car, I didn't stop to ________ how I'd pay for it.

a. consider
b. promote
c. require
d. adjust

286. Kamala was the most intelligent person in the group, even though she had never had the ________ to attend college.

a. sensitivity
b. arrogance
c. opportunity
d. marketability

287. We knew nothing about Betty, because she was so ________.

a. expressive
b. secretive
c. emotional
d. artistic

Rhesus monkeys use facial expressions to communicate with each other and to enforce social order. For example, the "fear grimace," although it looks ferocious, is actually given by a ________ monkey who is intimidated by a ________ member of the group.

288. What is the meaning of the word grimace as it is used in the passage?

a. wrinkle
b. contortion
c. shriek
d. simper

289. Which pair of words or phrases, if inserted into the blanks in sequence, makes the most sense in the context of the passage?

a. calm . . . aggressive
b. dominant . . . subordinate
c. confident . . . fearless
d. subordinate . . . dominant

In protracted space flight, besides the obvious hazards of meteors, rocky debris, and radiation, astronauts will have to deal with muscle atrophy brought on by weightlessness; therefore, when they return to earth they will face a protracted period of weight-training to rebuild their strength.

290. What is the most likely meaning of the word debris as it is used in this passage?

a. fragments
b. decay
c. bacteria
d. alien life

291. The word atrophy as used in the paragraph most nearly means

a. pain
b. wasting
c. weakening
d. cramping

SET 40 (Answers begin on page 163.)

Looking at the author's word choice will help you arrive, not only at the literal meaning of the overall passage, but also at the correct inferences to be made from the passage. In addition, word choice will help you judge the writer's attitude toward the subject and let you know whether what is being presented is fact or opinion.

Some people avoid secretarial work because they picture themselves languishing at a dull job in a huge, impersonal corporation (their days enlivened only by being shouted at by a boss from Hell). Not all office work is traditional and dull, however—you may be lucky enough to land a position in a quirky little entrepreneurial office, run by an eccentric but entertaining manager.

292. What is the meaning of the underlined slang word quirky as it is used in the sentence?

a. nontraditional
b. shaky
c. careless
d. ludicrous

The Sami are an indigenous people living in the northern parts of Norway, Sweden, Finland, and Russia's Kola peninsula. Originally, the Sami religion was animistic; that is, for them, nature and natural objects had a conscious life, a spirit. One was expected to move quietly in the wilderness and avoid making a disturbance out of courtesy to these spirits. Ghengis Khan is said to have declared that the Sami were one people he would never try to fight again. Since the Sami were not warriors and did not believe in war, they simply disappeared in times of conflict. They were known as "peaceful retreaters."

293. Based on the tone of the passage, which of the following words best describes the author's attitude toward the Sami people?

a. admiring
b. pitying
c. contemptuous
d. patronizing

294. The closest meaning of the word underlined word animistic, as it is used in the passage, is

a. the irrational belief in supernatural beings
b. the belief that animals and plants have souls
c. the belief that animals are gods
d. the primitive belief that people can be reincarnated as animals

295. What is the meaning of the underlined word courtesy as it is used in the passage?

a. timidity
b. caution
c. respect
d. fear

SET 41 (Answers begin on page 164.)

Most paragraphs are organized (some obviously, some more subtly) around specific subjects. A sentence that sums up the paragraph is called the *topic sentence*. What's true of main idea questions is also true of topic sentence questions: You should pick one that makes an assertion general enough to encompass the idea of the whole paragraph. For the next three questions, choose the topic sentence that best fits the paragraph.

296. The term "overdose" is difficult to define. A single aspirin may cause hemorrhage in one person, while an injection of cocaine may merely make another high. ______________ ______________. Aspects such as age, weight, and general health are vitally important.

a. Drugs are an increasingly profound problem in society, one that most law enforcement officials simply aren't equipped to deal with.
b. Therefore, when dealing with an unconscious victim suspected of having overdosed, one must weigh certain factors carefully.
c. The 911 system, now available almost everywhere, is an invaluable tool in getting help to the victim of overdose.
d. Both aspirin and cocaine can look like harmless white powder, yet they are very different from one another in effect.

297. The term "spices" is a pleasant one, whether it connotes fine French cuisine or a down-home, cinnamon-flavored apple pie. ______________ ______________. Individuals have traveled the world seeking exotic spices for profit and, in searching, have changed the course of history. Indeed, to gain control of lands harboring new spices, nations have actually gone to war.

a. The taste and aroma of spices are the main elements that make food such a source of fascination and pleasure.
b. The term might equally bring to mind Indian curry made thousands of miles away and those delicious barbecued ribs sold down on the corner.
c. It is exciting to find a good cookbook and experiment with spices from other lands—indeed, it is one way to travel around the globe!
d. The history of spices, however, is another matter altogether, often exciting, at times filled with danger and intrigue.

298. It weighs less than three pounds and is hardly more interesting to look at than an overly ripe cauliflower. ______________ ______________. It has created poetry and music, planned and executed horrific wars, devised intricate scientific theories. It thinks and dreams, plots and schemes, and easily holds more information than all the libraries on earth.

a. Yet the human brain is made of gelatinous matter and contains no nerve endings whatever.
b. Yet the science of neurology has found a way to map the most important areas of the human brain.
c. Yet the human brain is the most mysterious and complex object on earth.
d. Yet scientists say that each person uses use only ten percent of his or her brain over the course of a lifetime!

SET 42 (Answers begin on page 164.)

Topic sentences aren't magic. Some paragraphs don't even have an obvious topic sentence. Still, looking for the topic sentence is a good tool to use, among many others you have available, for ferreting out the meaning of a reading passage. For the three questions below, a topic sentence is given. Try choosing the sentence that best develops it.

299. Life on earth is ancient and, even at its first appearance, unimaginably complex.

a. Scientists place its beginnings at some 3000 million years ago, when the first molecule floated up out of the ooze with the unique ability to replicate itself.

b. The most complex life form is, of course, the mammal—and the most complex mammal is us.

c. It is unknown exactly where life started, where the first molecule was "born" that had the ability to replicate itself.

d. Darwin's Theory of Evolution was one attempt to explain what essentially remains a great mystery.

300. The continuing fascination of the public with movie star Marilyn Monroe is puzzling, yet it is still strong, even after four decades.

a. She became a star in the 1950s and died in 1962.

b. The film that most clearly demonstrates her talent is *The Misfits.*

c. Her name was originally "Norma Jeane," but she changed it to "Marilyn."

d. One reason might simply be her life's sad and premature end.

301. One scientific theory of the origin of the universe is the much-misunderstood Big Bang theory.

a. Physicists now believe they can construct what happened in the universe during the first three minutes of its beginnings.

b. Many scientists believe that, during microwave experiments, we can actually "hear" echoes of the Big Bang.

c. The popular notion is that the Big Bang was a huge explosion in space, but this is far too simple a description.

d. The Big Bang theory, if accepted, convinces us that the universe was not always as it is now.

SET 43 (Answers begin on page 164.)

Try your hand at these longer passages, which contain technical and scientific information, much of it related to medicine. These sets will ask you to dig out information from a large block of text, and it will further test your ability to define words from their context. The paragraphs are numbered for convenience.

(1) A government report addressing concerns about the many implications of genetic testing outlined policy guidelines and legislative recommendations intended to avoid involuntary and ineffective testing and to protect confidentiality. The report identified urgent concerns, such as quality control measures (including federal oversight for testing laboratories) and better genetics training for medical practitioners. It recommended voluntary screening; urged couples in high-risk populations to consider carrier screening; and advised caution in using and interpreting pre-symptomatic or predictive tests as certain information could easily be misused or misinterpreted.

(2) About three in every 100 children are born with a severe disorder presumed to be genetic or partially genetic in origin. Genes, often in concert with environmental factors, are being linked to the causes of many common adult diseases such as coronary artery disease, hypertension, various cancers, diabetes, and Alzheimer's disease. Tests to determine <u>predisposition</u> to a variety of conditions are under study, and some are beginning to be applied.

(3) The report recommended that all screening, including screening of newborns, be voluntary. Citing the results of two different voluntary newborn screening programs, the report said these programs can achieve compliance rates equal to or better than those of mandatory programs. State health departments could eventually mandate the offering of tests for diagnosing treatable conditions in newborns; however, careful pilot studies for conditions diagnosable at birth need to be done first.

(4) Although the report asserted that it would prefer that all screening be voluntary, it did note that if a state requires newborn screening for a particular condition, the state should do so only if there is strong evidence that a newborn would benefit from effective treatment at the earliest possible age. Newborn screening is the most common type of genetic screening today. More than four million newborns are tested annually so that effective treatment can be started in a few hundred infants.

(5) Prenatal testing can pose the most difficult issues. The ability to diagnose genetic disorders in the fetus far exceeds any ability to treat or cure them. Parents must be fully informed about risks and benefits of testing procedures, the nature and variability of the disorders they would disclose, and the options available if test results are positive.

(6) Obtaining informed consent—a process that would include educating participants, not just processing documents—would enhance voluntary participation. When offered testing, parents should receive comprehensive counseling, which should be nondirective. Relevant medical advice, however, is recommended for treatable or preventable conditions.

(7) Genetics also can predict whether certain diseases might develop later in life. For single-gene diseases, population screening should only be considered for treatable or preventable conditions of relatively high frequency. Children should be tested only for disorders for which effective treatments or preventive measures could be applied early in life.

302. As it is used in paragraph 2, the underlined word predisposition most nearly means

a. willingness
b. susceptibility
c. impartiality
d. composure

303. The report stressed the need for caution in the use and interpretation of

a. predictive tests
b. newborn screening
c. informed consent
d. pilot studies

304. According to the passage, how many infants are treated for genetic disorders as a result of newborn screening?

a. dozens
b. hundreds
c. thousands
d. millions

305. One intention of the policy guidelines was to

a. implement compulsory testing
b. minimize concerns about quality control
c. endorse the expansion of screening programs
d. preserve privacy in testing

306. According to the report, states should implement mandatory infant screening only

a. if the compliance rate for voluntary screening is low
b. for mothers who are at high risk for genetic disease
c. after meticulous research is undertaken
d. to avoid the abuse of sensitive information

307. The most prevalent form of genetic testing is conducted

a. on high-risk populations
b. on adults
c. on fetuses prior to birth
d. on infants shortly after birth

SET 44 (Answers begin on page 164.)

While it's not a rule, many times in scientific and technical passages, material that looks daunting because of unfamiliar vocabulary is actually straightforward and explicit. Active reading skills are needed, but they are no different from the skills needed when you're dealing with simpler text.

(1) By using tiny probes as neural prostheses, scientists may be able to restore nerve function in quadriplegics and make the blind see or the deaf hear. Thanks to advanced techniques, a single, small, implanted probe can stimulate individual neurons electrically or chemically and then record responses. Preliminary results suggest that the microprobe telemetry systems can be permanently implanted and replace damaged or missing nerves.

(2) The tissue-compatible microprobes represent an advance over the typical aluminum wire electrodes used in studies of the cortex and other brain structures. Researchers accumulate much data using traditional electrodes, but there is a question of how much damage they cause to the nervous system. Microprobes, which are about as thin as a human hair, cause minimal damage and disruption of neurons when inserted into the brain.

(3) In addition to recording nervous system impulses, the microprobes have minuscule channels that open the way for delivery of drugs, cellular growth factors, neurotransmitters, and other neuroactive compounds to a single neuron or to groups of neurons. Also, patients who lack certain biochemicals could receive doses via prostheses. The probes can have up to four channels, each with its own recording/stimulating electrode.

308. One similar feature of microprobes and wire electrodes is
- a. a minimal disturbance of neurons
- b. the density of the material
- c. the capacity for multiple leads
- d. their ability to generate information

309. Which of the following best expresses the main idea of the passage?
- a. Microprobes require further technological advances before they can be used in humans.
- b. Wire electrodes are antiquated as a means for delivering neuroactive compounds to the brain.
- c. Microprobes have great potential to help counteract neural damage.
- d. Technology now exists that may enable repair of the nervous system.

310. All of the following are mentioned in the passage as potential uses for prostheses EXCEPT
- a. transportation of medication
- b. induction of physical movement
- c. transportation of growth factor
- d. removal of biochemicals from the cortex

311. The initial function of microprobe channels is to
- a. create pathways
- b. disrupt neurons
- c. replace ribbon cables
- d. study the brain

SET 45 (Answers begin on page 165.)

It's natural to feel overwhelmed when faced with unfamiliar subjects and with terms you may not have heard before. Just relax and remember that the reading process is the same whether the text is long or short, complex or simple. Read closely and carefully. Underline, take notes. Try outlining the passage.

(1) Medical waste has been a growing concern because of recent incidents of public exposure to discarded blood vials, needles (sharps), empty prescription bottles, and syringes. Medical waste can typically include general refuse, human blood and blood products, cultures and stocks of infectious agents, laboratory animal carcasses, contaminated bedding material, and pathological wastes.

(2) Wastes are generally collected by gravity chutes, carts, or pneumatic tubes, each of which has its own advantages and disadvantages. Chutes are limited to vertical transport, and there is some risk of exhausting contaminants into hallways if a door is left open during use. Another disadvantage of gravity chutes is that the waste container may get jammed while dropping or broken upon hitting the bottom. Carts are primarily for horizontal transport of bagged or containerized wastes. The main risk here is that bags may be broken or torn during transport, potentially exposing the worker to the wastes. Using automated carts can reduce the potential for exposure. Pneumatic tubes offer the best performance for waste transport in a large facility. Advantages include high-speed movement, movement in any direction, and minimal intermediate storage of untreated wastes. However, some objects cannot be conveyed pneumatically.

(3) Off-site disposal of regulated medical wastes remains a viable option for smaller hospitals (those with less than 150 beds). Some preliminary on-site processing, such as compaction or hydropulping, may be necessary prior to sending the waste off-site. Compaction reduces the total volume of solid wastes, often reducing transportation and disposal costs, but does not change the hazardous characteristics of the waste. However, compaction may not be economical if transportation and disposal costs are based on weight rather than volume.

(4) Hydropulping involves grinding the waste in the presence of an oxidizing fluid, such as hypochlorite solution. The liquid is separated from the pulp and discharged directly into the sewer unless local limits require additional pretreatment prior to discharge. The pulp can often be disposed of at a landfill. One advantage is that waste can be rendered innocuous and reduced in size within the same system. Disadvantages are the added operating burden, difficulty of controlling fugitive emissions, and the difficulty of conducting microbiological tests to determine whether all organic matters and infectious organisms from the waste have been destroyed.

(5) On-site disposal is a feasible alternative for hospitals generating two tons per day or more of total solid waste. Common treatment techniques include steam sterilization and incineration. Although other options are available, incineration is currently the preferred method for on-site treatment of hospital waste.

(6) Steam sterilization is limited in the types of medical waste it can treat but is appropriate for laboratory cultures and/or substances contaminated with infectious organisms. The waste is subjected to steam in a sealed, pressurized chamber. The liquid that may form is drained off to the sewer or sent for processing. The unit is then reopened after a vapor release to the atmosphere, and the solid waste is taken out for further processing or disposal. One advantage of steam sterilization is that it has been used for many years in hospitals to sterilize instruments and containers and to treat small quantities of waste. However, since sterili-

zation does not change the appearance of the waste, there could be a problem in gaining acceptance of the waste for landfilling.

(7) A properly designed, maintained, and operated incinerator achieves a relatively high level of organism destruction. Incineration reduces the weight and volume of the waste as much as 95 percent and is especially appropriate for pathological wastes and sharps. The most common incineration system for medical waste is the controlled-air type. The principal advantage of this type of incinerator is low particulate emissions. Rotary kiln and grate type units have been used, but use of grate type units has been discontinued due to high air emissions. The rotary kiln also puts out high emissions, and the costs have been prohibitive for smaller units.

312. Which of the following organizational schemes is most prevalent in the passage?

a. chronological order
b. comparison-contrast
c. order by topic
d. hierarchical order

313. One disadvantage of the compaction method of waste disposal is that it

a. cannot reduce transportation costs
b. reduces the volume of solid waste material
c. does not allow hospitals to confirm that organic matter has been eliminated
d. does not reduce the weight of solid waste material

314. For hospitals that dispose of waste on their own premises, the optimum treatment method is

a. incineration
b. compaction
c. sterilization
d. hydropulping

315. According to the passage, which of the following could be safely disposed of in a landfill but might not be accepted by landfill facilities?

a. hydropulped material
b. sterilized waste
c. incinerated waste
d. laboratory cultures

316. The two processes mentioned in the passage that involve the formation of liquid are

a. compaction and hydropulping
b. incineration and compaction
c. hydropulping and sterilization
d. sterilization and incineration

317. According to the passage, two effective methods for treating waste caused by infectious matter are

a. steam sterilization and incineration
b. hydropulping and steam sterilization
c. incineration and compaction
d. hydropulping and incineration

318. Hospitals can minimize employee contact with dangerous waste by switching from

a. a manual cart to a gravity chute
b. an automated cart to a hydropulping machine
c. a gravity chute to a manual cart
d. a manual cart to an automated cart

319. The process that transforms waste from hazardous to harmless AND diminishes waste volume is

a. sterilization
b. hydropulping
c. oxidizing
d. compacting

320. The underlined word exhausting, as it is used in the second paragraph of the passage, most nearly means

a. debilitating
b. disregarding
c. detonating
d. discharging

321. Budgetary constraints have precluded some small hospitals from purchasing

a. pneumatic tubes
b. rotary kilns
c. sterilization equipment
d. controlled-air kilns

322. The underlined phrase fugitive emissions in the fourth paragraph most nearly means

a. contaminants that are extremely toxic
b. contaminants that are illegally discharged
c. contaminants that escape the disposal process
d. contaminants that come from microbiological testing

SET 46 (Answers begin on page 166.)

Isolate the unfamiliar words as you read, by underlining them or jotting them down. Then go back and look at the sentences before and after them—that is, at their immediate context.

(1) Spina bifida is a defect of the spinal column that occurs during the first 28 days after fertilization of a human ovum. It is the condition in which the bones of the spinal column surrounding the spinal cord do not close properly, and the cord or spinal fluid bulges through a section of the lower back. Any portion of the spinal cord outside the vertebrae is undeveloped or damaged and will inevitably cause paralysis and incontinence. However, there is a minor and a major form of this condition. The symptom of the mild form, called spina bifida *occulta* ("hidden"), is a small gap in the spine covered by a dimple in the skin. This condition can be so mild that some people who have spina bifida occulta may never even know they have it.

(2) In contrast, the more disabling form, called spina bifida *aperta*, is what most people refer to as spina bifida. On rare occasions, spina bifida aperta results in a small but noticeable sac called a meningocle forming on the fetus' back. The meningocle may be repaired after birth in a major surgical procedure. Afterwards, the patient may suffer little or no muscle paralysis. However, in 90 percent of all spina bifida aperta cases, a portion of the undeveloped spinal cord itself protrudes through the spine and forms a sac. This so-called myelocele (or meningomyelocele) is visible on the baby's back. The location of the myelocele determines how severely disabled the child will be. In general, the higher it is on the spinal column, the more paralysis is possible. Doctors must repair any opening of the spine shortly after birth or the child will die. Other major surgeries often follow in the child's first years.

(3) Depending on the severity of their condition, children with spina bifida have varying degrees of paralysis and incontinence. About 85 percent of them develop hydrocephalus, an accumulation of cerebrospinal fluid surrounding the brain. This fluid must be drained to the abdomen or blood stream with a surgically implanted tube. Some children with spina bifida develop foot and knee deformities caused by an interruption of spinal nerve circuits. Many patients require leg braces, crutches, and other devices to help them walk. They may have learning disabilities, and about 30 percent of these children have slight to severe mental retardation. Other results of this condition are chronic bladder infections and kidney problems, which require lifelong medical attention. Despite their need for medical attention, children with spina bifida can learn to care for many of their own needs and lead productive lives. While once all of these children died, with proper medical treatment, between 85 and 90 percent of them now live to adulthood.

323. Which statement is true of the majority of spina bifida aperta cases?
a. The only noticeable symptom is an indentation in the skin on the patient's back.
b. A part of the undeveloped spinal cord forms a myelocele protruding from the back.
c. About 85 percent of children with spina bifida aperta die following surgery.
d. Most children with spina bifida aperta have fewer symptoms than children with spina bifida occulta.

324. All of the following are mentioned in the passage as results of spina bifida EXCEPT
a. learning disabilities
b. chronic bladder infections
c. foot and knee deformities
d. hyperactivity

325. The human vertebral column consists of the following groups of vertebrae, listed here from the highest, or top, down to the lowest, or bottom, of the spinal column: the cervical vertebrae, the thoracic vertebrae, the lumbar vertebrae, the sacrum, and the coccyx. On which vertebrae group would a myelocele cause the most severe disability?

a. the thoracic vertebrae
b. the sacrum
c. the cervical vertebrae
d. the lumbar vertebrae

326. What is the term for a pool of cerebrospinal fluid in the area around the brain?

a. catheterization
b. spina bifida
c. hydrocephalus
d. meningomyelocele

327. Which of the following is the small sac that may result in little or no muscle paralysis or incontinence after being repaired?

a. meningocele
b. myelocele
c. meningomyelocele
d. aperta

328. The conclusion of this passage could best be summarized by which of the following statements?

a. All pregnant women should have their fetuses tested for spina bifida.
b. Infants with spina bifida should be allowed to die with dignity.
c. Spina bifida is a birth defect that kills millions of innocent children each year.
d. People who have spina bifida may lead productive lives with proper medical attention.

329. Given the discussion of spina bifida, what is the most likely meaning of the root word bifid?

a. hardened or brittle
b. embryonic
c. cleft or split
d. reversed

SET 47 (Answers begin on page 166.)

First read the passage in a relaxed manner to get a sense of its overall meaning and organizational pattern. After that, go back and take the passage a paragraph or even a few sentences at a time. A block of text that at first seems overwhelming can be less so if considered in smaller chunks.

(1) The atmosphere forms a gaseous, protective envelope around earth. It protects earth from the cold of space, from harmful ultraviolet light, and from all but the largest meteors. After traveling over 93 million miles, solar energy strikes the atmosphere and earth's surface, warming the planet and creating what is known as the "biosphere," which is the region of earth capable of sustaining life. Solar radiation in combination with the planet's rotation causes the atmosphere to circulate. Atmospheric circulation is one important reason that life on earth can exist at higher latitudes because equatorial heat is transported poleward, moderating the climate.

(2) The equatorial region is the warmest part of the earth because it receives the most direct and therefore strongest solar radiation. The plane in which the earth revolves around the sun is called the ecliptic. Earth's axis is inclined $23\frac{1}{2}$ degrees with respect to the ecliptic. This inclined axis is responsible for our changing seasons because, as seen from the earth, the sun oscillates back and forth across the equator in an annual cycle. About June 21 each year the sun reaches the Tropic of Cancer, $23\frac{1}{2}$ degrees north latitude. This is the northernmost point where the sun can be directly overhead. About December 21 of each year the sun reaches the Tropic of Capricorn, $23\frac{1}{2}$ degrees south latitude. This is the southernmost point at which the sun can be directly overhead. The polar regions are the coldest parts of the earth because they receive the least direct and therefore the weakest solar radiation. Here solar radiation strikes at a very oblique angle and thus spreads the same amount of energy over a greater area than in the equatorial regions. A static envelope of air surrounding the earth would produce an extremely hot, unlivable equatorial region while the polar regions would remain unlivably cold.

(3) The transport of water vapor in the atmosphere is an important mechanism by which heat energy is redistributed poleward. When water evaporates into the air and becomes water vapor it absorbs energy. At the equator, water vapor-saturated air rises high into the atmosphere where winds aloft carry it poleward. As this moist air approaches the polar regions it cools and sinks back to earth. At some point the water vapor condenses out of the air as rain or snow, releasing energy in the process. The now dry polar air flows back toward the equator to repeat the convection cycle. In this way, heat energy absorbed at the equator is deposited at the poles and the temperature gradient between these regions is reduced.

(4) The circulation of the atmosphere and the weather it generates is but one example of the many complex, interdependent events of nature. The web of life depends on the proper functioning of these natural mechanisms for its continued existence. Global warming, the hole in the atmosphere's ozone layer, and increasing air and water pollution pose serious, long term threats to the biosphere. Given the high degree of nature's interconnectedness, it is quite possible that the most serious threats have yet to be recognized.

330. Which of the following best expresses the main idea of the passage?

a. The circulation of atmosphere—now threatened by global warming, the hole in the ozone layer, and pollution—protects the biosphere and makes life on earth possible.
b. If the protective atmosphere around the earth is too damaged by human activity, all life on earth will cease.
c. Life on earth is the result of complex interdependent events of nature, events which are being interfered with at the current time by harmful human activity.
d. The circulation of atmosphere is the single most important factor in keeping the biosphere alive, and it is constantly threatened by harmful human activity.

331. Which of the following best represents the organization of the passage?

a. I. Definition and description of the circulation of the atmosphere.
   II. How the atmosphere affects heat and water in the biosphere.
   III. How the circulation of the atmosphere works.
   IV. What will happen if human activity destroys the atmosphere and other life-sustaining mechanisms.
b. I. Origin of the atmosphere and ways it protects the biosphere.
   II. How the circulation of the atmosphere affects the equator and the poles.
   III. How the circulation of the atmosphere interrelates with other events in nature to protect life on earth.
   IV. Threats to life in the biosphere.
c. I. Definition and description of the circulation of the atmosphere.
   II. Protective functions of the circulation of the atmosphere.
   III. Relationship of the circulation of the atmosphere to other life-sustaining mechanisms.
   IV. Threats to the nature's interconnectedness in the biosphere.
d. I. The journey of the atmosphere 93 million miles through space.
   II. How the atmosphere circulates and protects the biosphere.
   III. How the atmosphere interrelates with weather in the biosphere.
   IV. How damage to the biosphere threatens life on earth.

332. Which of the following is the best definition of "biosphere" as it is used in the passage?
a. the protective envelope formed by the atmosphere around the living earth
b. that part of the earth and its atmosphere in which life can exist
c. the living things on earth whose existence is made possible by circulation of the atmosphere
d. the circulation of the atmosphere's contribution to life on earth

333. Which of the following sentences from the passage best supports the author's point that circulation of the atmosphere is vital to life on earth?
a. "The equatorial region is the warmest part of the earth because it receives the most direct and therefore strongest solar radiation."
b. "The circulation of the atmosphere and the weather it generates is but one example of the many complex, interdependent events of nature."
c. "[The atmosphere] protects earth from the cold of space, from harmful ultraviolet light, and from all but the largest meteors."
d. "A static envelope of air surrounding the earth would produce an unlivably hot equatorial region while the polar regions would remain unlivably cold."

334. Based on the passage, which of the following is directly responsible for all temperature changes on earth?
a. variations in the strength of solar radiation
b. variations in the amount of ultraviolet light
c. variation of biologic processes in the biosphere
d. variation in global warming

335. The first paragraph of the passage deals mainly with which of the following effects of the atmosphere on the earth.
a. its sheltering effect
b. its reviving effect
c. its invigorating effect
d. its cleansing effect

SET 48 (Answers begin on page 167.)

Scientific language is precise and concrete, so never just throw up your hands when confronted with it. Take an active part in the reading process. When you come upon a word you don't know, remember to look closely at the context.

(1) There are two types of diabetes, insulin-dependent and non-insulin-dependent. Between 90 and 95 percent of the estimated 13 to 14 million people in the United States with diabetes have non-insulin-dependent, or Type II, diabetes. Because this form of diabetes usually begins in adults over the age of 40 and is most common after the age of 55, it used to be called adult-onset diabetes. Its symptoms often develop gradually and are hard to identify at first; therefore, nearly half of all people with diabetes do not know they have it. For instance, someone who has developed Type II diabetes may feel tired or ill without knowing why. This can be particularly dangerous because untreated diabetes can cause damage to the heart, blood vessels, eyes, kidneys, and nerves. While the causes, short-term effects, and treatments of the two types of diabetes differ, both types can cause the same long-term health problems.

(2) Most importantly, both types affect the body's ability to use digested food for energy. Diabetes does not interfere with digestion, but it does prevent the body from using an important product of digestion, glucose (commonly known as sugar), for energy. After a meal, the normal digestive system breaks some food down into glucose. The blood carries the glucose or sugar throughout the body, causing blood glucose levels to rise. In response to this rise, the hormone insulin is released into the bloodstream and signals the body tissues to metabolize or burn the glucose for fuel, which causes blood glucose levels to return to normal. The glucose that the body does not use right away is stored in the liver, muscle, or fat.

(3) In both types of diabetes, however, this normal process malfunctions. A gland called the pancreas, found just behind the stomach, makes insulin. In people with insulin-dependent diabetes, the pancreas does not produce insulin at all. This condition usually begins in childhood and is known as Type I (formerly called juvenile-onset) diabetes. These patients must have daily insulin injections to survive. People with non-insulin-dependent diabetes usually produce some insulin in their pancreas, but the body's tissues do not respond very well to the insulin signal and therefore do not metabolize the glucose properly, a condition known as insulin resistance.

(4) Insulin resistance is an important factor in non-insulin-dependent diabetes, and scientists are searching for the causes of insulin resistance. They have identified two possibilities. The first is that there could be a defect in the insulin receptors on cells. Like an appliance that needs to be plugged into an electrical outlet, insulin has to bind to a receptor in order to function. Several things can go wrong with receptors. For example, there may not be enough receptors for insulin to bind to, or a defect in the receptors may prevent insulin from binding. The second possible cause of insulin resistance is that, although insulin may bind to the receptors, the cells do not read the signal to metabolize the glucose. Scientists continue to study these cells to see why this might happen.

(5) There's no cure for diabetes yet. However, there are ways to alleviate its symptoms. In 1986, a National Institutes of Health panel of experts recommended that the best treatment for non-insulin-dependent diabetes is a diet that helps one maintain a normal weight and pays particular attention to a proper balance of the different food groups. Many experts, including those in the American Diabetes Association, recommend that

50 to 60 percent of daily calories come from carbohydrates, 12 to 20 percent from protein, and no more than 30 percent from fat. Foods that are rich in carbohydrates, like breads, cereals, fruits, and vegetables break down into glucose during digestion, causing blood glucose to rise. Additionally, studies have shown that cooked foods raise blood glucose higher than raw, unpeeled foods. A doctor or nutritionist should always be consulted for more of this kind of information and for help in planning a diet to offset the effects of this form of diabetes.

336. According to the passage, what may be the most dangerous aspect of Type II diabetes?
a. Insulin shots are needed daily for treatment of Type II diabetes.
b. Type II diabetes may go undetected and therefore untreated.
c. In Type II diabetes the pancreas does not produce insulin.
d. Type II diabetes interferes with digestion.

337. Which of the following are the same for Type I and Type II diabetes?
a. treatments
b. long-term health risks
c. short-term effects
d. causes

338. According to the passage, one place in which excess glucose is stored is the
a. stomach
b. insulin receptors
c. pancreas
d. liver

339. A diet dominated by which of the following is recommended for non-insulin-dependent diabetics?
a. protein
b. fat
c. carbohydrates
d. raw foods

340. Which of the following is the main function of insulin?
a. It signals tissues to metabolize sugar.
b. It breaks down food into glucose.
c. It carries glucose throughout the body.
d. It binds to receptors.

341. Which of the following statements best summarizes the main theme of the passage?
a. Type I and Type II diabetes are best treated by maintaining a high protein diet.
b. Type II diabetes is a distinct condition that can be managed by maintaining a healthy diet.
c. Type I diabetes is an insidious condition most harmful when the patient is not taking daily insulin injections.
d. Adults who suspect they may have Type II diabetes should immediately adopt a high carbohydrate diet.

342. Which of the following is mentioned in the passage as a possible problem with insulin receptors in insulin-resistant individuals?

a. Overeating causes the receptors not to function properly.
b. There may be an overabundance of receptors present.
c. A defect causes the receptors to bind with glucose.
d. A defect hinders the receptors from binding with insulin.

343. According to the passage, in normal individuals, which of the following processes occur immediately after the digestive system converts some food into glucose?

a. The glucose is metabolized by body tissues.
b. Insulin is released into the bloodstream.
c. Blood sugar levels rise.
d. The pancreas manufactures increased amounts of insulin.

344. Based on the information in the passage, which of the following best describes people with Type I diabetes?

a. They do not need to be treated with injections of insulin.
b. They comprise the majority of people with diabetes.
c. Their pancreases do not produce insulin.
d. They are usually diagnosed as adults.

345. What is the closest meaning of the underlined word offset in the final sentence of the passage?

a. counteract
b. cure
c. soothe
d. erase

SET 49 (Answers begin on page 167.)

Remember that much scientific and technical writing deals with cold, hard, *explicit* facts. This means that, with close reading, you stand a good chance of answering most, if not all, of the questions with confidence.

No longer is asthma considered a condition with isolated, acute episodes of bronchospasm. Rather, asthma is now understood to be a chronic inflammatory disorder of the airways—that is, inflammation makes the airways chronically sensitive. When these hyperresponsive airways are irritated, air flow is limited, and attacks of coughing, wheezing, chest tightness, and difficulty breathing occur.

Asthma involves complex interactions among inflammatory cells, mediators, and the cells and tissues in the airways. The interactions result in airflow limitation from acute bronchoconstriction, swelling of the airway wall, increased mucus secretion, and airway remodeling. The inflammation also causes an increase in airway responsiveness. During an asthma attack, the patient attempts to compensate by breathing at a higher lung volume in order to keep the air flowing through the constricted airways, and the greater the airway limitation, the higher the lung volume must be to keep airways open. The morphologic changes that occur in asthma include bronchial infiltration by inflammatory cells. Key effector cells in the inflammatory response are the mast cells, T lymphocytes, and eosinophils. Mast cells and eosinophils are also significant participants in allergic responses, hence the similarities between allergic reactions and asthma attacks. Other changes include mucus plugging of the airways, interstitial edema, and microvascular leakage. Destruction of bronchial epithelium and thickening of the subbasement membrane is also characteristic. In addition, there may be hypertrophy and hyperplasia of airway smooth muscle, increase in goblet cell number, and enlargement of submucous glands.

Although causes of the initial tendency toward inflammation in the airways of patients with asthma are not yet certain, to date the strongest identified risk factor is atopy. This inherited familial tendency to have allergic reactions includes increased sensitivity to allergens that are risk factors for developing asthma. Some of these allergens include domestic dust mites, animals with fur, cockroaches, pollens, and molds. Additionally, asthma may be triggered by viral respiratory infections, especially in children. By avoiding these allergens and triggers, a person with asthma lowers his or her risk of irritating sensitive airways. A few avoidance techniques include keeping the home clean and well-ventilated, using an air conditioner in the summer months when pollen and mold counts are high, and getting an annual influenza vaccination. Of course, asthma sufferers should avoid tobacco smoke altogether. Cigar, cigarette, or pipe smoke is a trigger whether the patient smokes or breathes in the smoke from others. Smoke increases the risk of allergic sensitization in children, and increases the severity of symptoms in children who already have asthma and may be fatal. Many of the risk factors for developing asthma may also provoke asthma attacks, and people with asthma may have one or more triggers, which vary from individual to individual. The risk can be further reduced by taking medications that decrease airway inflammation. Most <u>exacerbations</u> can be prevented by the combination of avoiding triggers and taking anti-inflammatory medications. An exception is physical activity, which is a common trigger of exacerbations in asthma patients. However, asthma patients should not necessarily avoid all physical exertion, because some types of activity have been proven to reduce symptoms. Rather, they should work in conjunction with a doctor to design a proper training regimen including the use of medication.

In order to diagnose asthma, a health care professional must appreciate the underlying disorder that leads to asthma symptoms and understand how to recognize the condition through information gathered from the patient's history, physical examination, measurements of lung function, and allergic status. Because asthma symptoms vary throughout the day, the respiratory system may appear normal during physical examination. Clinical signs are more likely to be present when a patient is experiencing symptoms; however, the absence of symptoms at the time of the examination does not exclude the diagnosis of asthma.

346. According to the passage, what is the name for the familial inclination to have hypersensitivity to certain allergens?
a. interstitial edema
b. hyperplasia
c. hypertrophy
d. atopy

347. Why does a person suffering from an asthma attack attempt to inhale more air?
a. to prevent the loss of consciousness
b. to keep air flowing through shrunken air passageways
c. to prevent hyperplasia
d. to compensate for weakened mast cells, T lymphocytes, and eosinophils

348. The passage suggests that in the past asthma was regarded as which of the following?
a. a result of the overuse of tobacco products
b. an hysterical condition
c. mysterious, unrelated attacks affecting the lungs
d. a chronic condition

349. Which of the following would be the best replacement for the underlined word exacerbations in this passage?
a. allergies
b. attacks
c. triggers
d. allergens

350. The passage mentions all of the following bodily changes during an asthma attack EXCEPT
a. severe cramping in the chest
b. heavy breathing
c. airways blocked by fluids
d. constricted airways

351. Which of the following triggers, albeit surprising, is mentioned in the passage as possibly reducing the symptoms of asthma in some patients?

a. using a fan instead of an air conditioner in summer months
b. exposure to second-hand cigarette smoke
c. the love of a family pet
d. performing physical exercise

352. Why might a patient with asthma have an apparently normal respiratory system during an examination by a doctor?

a. Asthma symptoms come and go throughout the day.
b. Severe asthma occurs only after strenuous physical exertion.
c. Doctors offices are smoke-free and very clean.
d. The pollen and mold count may be low that day.

353. Who might be the most logical audience for this passage?

a. researchers studying the respiratory system
b. health care professionals
c. a mother whose child has been diagnosed with asthma
d. an antismoking activist

354. What is the reason given in this article for why passive smoke should be avoided by children?

a. A smoke-filled room is a breeding ground for viral respiratory infections.
b. Smoke can stunt an asthmatic child's growth.
c. Smoke can heighten the intensity of asthma symptoms.
d. Breathing smoke can lead to a fatal asthma attack.

SET 50 (Answers begin on page 168.)

Remember to read the whole passage in a relaxed manner, then go back and work with it in small chunks. Take your time. Underline. Circle words. Take notes.

(1) The immune system is equal in complexity to the combined <u>intricacies</u> of the brain and nervous system. The success of the immune system in defending the body relies on a dynamic regulatory-communications network consisting of millions and millions of cells. Organized into sets and subsets, these cells pass information back and forth like clouds of bees swarming around a hive. The result is a sensitive system of checks and balances that produces an immune response that is prompt, appropriate, effective and self-limiting.

(2) At the heart of the immune system is the ability to distinguish between *self* and *nonself.* When immune defenders encounter cells or organisms carrying foreign or nonself molecules, the immune troops move quickly to eliminate the intruders. Virtually every body cell carries distinctive molecules that identify it as self. The body's immune defenses do not normally attack tissues that carry a self marker. Rather, immune cells and other body cells coexist peaceably in a state known as self-tolerance. When a normally functioning immune system attacks a nonself molecule, the system has the ability to "remember" the specifics of the foreign body. Upon subsequent encounters with the same species of molecules, the immune system reacts accordingly. With the possible exception of antibodies passed during lactation, this so-called immune system memory is not inherited. Despite the occurrence of a virus in your family, your immune system must "learn" from experience with the many millions of distinctive nonself molecules in the sea of microbes in which we live. Learning entails producing the appropriate molecules and cells to match up with and counteract each nonself invader.

(3) Any substance capable of triggering an immune response is called an *antigen.* Antigens are not to be confused with *allergens,* which are most often harmless substances (such as ragweed pollen or cat hair) that provoke the immune system to set off the inappropriate and harmful response known as allergy. An antigen can be a virus, a bacterium, a fungus, a parasite, or even a portion or product of one of these organisms. Tissues or cells from another individual (except an identical twin, whose cells carry identical self-markers) also act as antigens; because the immune system recognizes transplanted tissues as foreign, it rejects them. The body will even reject nourishing proteins unless they are first broken down by the digestive system into their primary, non-antigenic building blocks. An antigen announces its foreignness by means of intricate and characteristic shapes called *epitopes,* which protrude from its surface. Most antigens, even the simplest microbes, carry several different kinds of epitopes on their surface; some may even carry several hundred. Some epitopes will be more effective than others at stimulating an immune response. Only in abnormal situations does the immune system wrongly identify self as nonself and execute a misdirected immune attack. The result can be a so-called autoimmune disease such as rheumatoid arthritis or systemic lupus erythematosis. The painful side effects of these diseases are caused by a person's immune system actually attacking itself.

355. What is the analogy used to describe the communications network among the cells in the immune system?

a. the immune system's memory
b. immune troops eliminating intruders
c. bees swarming around a hive
d. a sea of microbes

356. The immune cells and other cells in the body coexist peaceably in a state known as
a. equilibrium
b. self-tolerance
c. harmony
d. tolerance

357. What is the specific term for the substance capable of triggering an inappropriate or harmful immune response to a harmless substance such as ragweed pollen?
a. antigen
b. microbe
c. allergen
d. autoimmune disease

358. How do the cells in the immune system recognize an antigen as "foreign" or "non-self?"
a. through an allergic response
b. through blood type
c. through fine hairs protruding from the antigen surface
d. through characteristic shapes on the antigen surface

359. After you have had the chicken pox, your immune system will be able to do all of the following EXCEPT
a. prevent your offspring from infection by the chicken pox virus
b. distinguish between your body cells and that of the chicken pox virus
c. "remember" previous experiences with the chicken pox virus
d. match up and counteract nonself molecules in the form of the chicken pox virus

360. Which of the following best expresses the main idea of this passage?
a. An antigen is any substance that triggers an immune response.
b. The basic function of the immune system is to distinguish between self and nonself.
c. One of the immune system's primary functions is the allergic response.
d. The human body presents an opportune habitat for microbes.

361. Why would tissue transplanted from father to daughter have a greater risk of being detected as foreign than a tissue transplanted between identical twins?
a. The age of the twins' tissue would be the same, and therefore less likely to be rejected.
b. The identical twin's tissue would carry the same self-markers and would therefore be less likely to be rejected.
c. The difference in the sex of the father and daughter would cause the tissue to be rejected by the daughter's immune system.
d. The twins' immune systems would "remember" the same encounters with childhood illnesses.

362. What is the meaning of the underlined word <u>intricacies</u> as it is used in the first sentence of the passage?
a. elaborate interconnections
b. confusion of pathways
c. inherent perplexity
d. comprehensive coverage

SET 51 (Answers begin on page 169.)

Unless you work in a medical field, this set will likely appear extremely difficult, or even impossible, and you may be tempted to skip it. It'll be a good exercise, though, to try to ferret out the answers to the questions as best you can. To fully comprehend this passage you'd probably need a medical dictionary. Don't worry if your understanding isn't perfect. Just approach the passage like a good detective looking for clues. Relax and enjoy the mental exercise.

(1) Recombinant DNA technology allows scientists to cut segments of DNA from one type of organism and combine them with the genes of a second organism. Also called genetic engineering, recombinant DNA technology is a method by which relatively simple organisms, such as bacteria or yeast, or even mammalian cells in culture, can be induced to make quantities of human proteins, including interferons or interleukins. This technology has enabled scientists to grow tobacco plants that produce monoclonal antibodies, and goats that secrete a clot-dissolving heart attack drug, tissue plasminogen activator (TPA), in their milk.

(2) Another facet of recombinant DNA technology involves gene therapy. The goal of this therapy is to replace defective genes, or to endow a cell with new capabilities. In 1989, the feasibility and safety of gene transfer was demonstrated when tumor-infiltrating lymphocytes (TILs) were extracted from a patient, equipped with a marker gene (so they could be tracked and monitored), and then reinjected into patients with advanced cancer. To deliver the gene into the TIL, the scientists used a virus, exploiting its natural tendency to invade cells. Before being used as a *vector*, the virus was altered so that it could not reproduce or cause disease. This experiment demonstrated that gene-modified cells could survive for long periods in the bloodstream and in tumor deposits without harm to the patient.

(3) The earliest attempts to use genes therapeutically focused on a form of severe combined immunodeficiency disease (SCID), which is caused by the lack of an enzyme due to a single abnormal gene. The gene for this enzyme—adenosine deaminase (ADA)—is delivered into the patient's T cells by a modified retrovirus. When the virus splices its genes into those of the T cells, it simultaneously introduces the gene for the missing enzyme. After the treated T cells begin to produce the missing enzyme, they are injected back into the patient.

(4) Gene therapy is now being used with some cancer patients. TILs reinforced with a gene for the antitumor cytokine known as tumor necrosis factor (TNF) have been administered to patients with advanced melanoma, a deadly form of skin cancer. Plans are under way to engineer a cancer "vaccine" designed to improve anti-cancer immune responses by taking small bits of tumor from patients with cancer, outfitting the tumor cells with genes for immune cell activating cytokines such as IL2, and reinjecting these gene-modified tumors into the patient. While the thought of reintroducing a cancerous tumor into a patient seems somewhat frightening, the enhanced immune response triggered by this technique may help prevent the recurrence of cancer.

363. What innate characteristic of viruses did researchers take advantage of in order to transport genes into TILs?
a. protective protein coat
b. affinity for invading cells
c. noncellular consistency
d. ability to produce DNA from RNA

364. According to the passage, SCID is caused by
a. an overabundance of monoclonal antibodies
b. an overabundance of tumor necrosis factor
c. a lack of tumor necrosis factor
d. a lack of adenosine deaminase

365. Why might cancer patients be leery of the prospect of a cancer "vaccine" as discussed in this passage?
a. Vaccine recipients will be reinjected with cancerous material.
b. The vaccine is derived from the tobacco plant.
c. The safety of genetic transfer has not yet been proven.
d. Genetic material from the *vector* could invade the vaccine recipient's bloodstream.

366. According to the passage, which of the following organisms have been employed by researchers to produce human proteins?
a. fungi
b. plankton
c. yeast
d. viruses

367. Adenosine deaminase (ADA) is transferred into the T cells of a patient via which of the following?
a. marker gene
b. TIL
c. interferon
d. modified retrovirus

368. The underlined term recombinant DNA technology is synonymous with
a. making quantities of human protein
b. genetic engineering
c. exploiting the natural tendency of viruses to invade cells
d. SCID

SET 52 (Answers begin on page 169.)

The subject matter of this passage will probably be much more familiar to you. However, remember that on most reading comprehension tests you will not have to have outside knowledge of the subject. Be careful to answer questions only on the basis of what is in the passage.

Millions of people in the United States are affected by eating disorders. More than 90 percent of those afflicted are adolescent or young adult women. While all eating disorders share some common manifestations, anorexia nervosa, bulimia nervosa, and binge eating each have distinctive symptoms and risks.

People who intentionally starve themselves (even while experiencing severe hunger pains) suffer from anorexia nervosa. The disorder, which usually begins around the time of puberty, involves extreme weight loss to at least 15 percent below the individual's normal body weight. Many people with the disorder look emaciated but are convinced they are overweight. In patients with anorexia nervosa, starvation can damage vital organs such as the heart and brain. To protect itself, the body shifts into slow gear: menstrual periods stop, blood pressure rates drop, and thyroid function slows. Excessive thirst and frequent urination may occur. Dehydration contributes to constipation, and reduced body fat leads to lowered body temperature and the inability to withstand cold. Mild anemia, swollen joints, reduced muscle mass, and light-headedness also commonly occur in anorexia nervosa.

Anorexia nervosa sufferers can exhibit sudden angry outbursts or become socially withdrawn. One in ten cases of anorexia nervosa leads to death from starvation, cardiac arrest, other medical complications, or suicide. Clinical depression and anxiety place many individuals with eating disorders at risk for suicidal behavior.

People with bulimia nervosa consume large amounts of food and then rid their bodies of the excess calories by vomiting, abusing laxatives or diuretics, taking enemas, or exercising obsessively. Some use a combination of all these forms of purging. Individuals with bulimia who use drugs to stimulate vomiting, bowel movements, or urination may be in considerable danger, as this practice increases the risk of heart failure. Dieting heavily between episodes of bingeing and purging is common.

Because many individuals with bulimia binge and purge in secret and maintain normal or above normal body weight, they can often successfully hide their problem for years. But bulimia nervosa patients—even those of normal weight—can severely damage their bodies by frequent binge eating and purging. In rare instances, binge eating causes the stomach to rupture; purging may result in heart failure due to loss of vital minerals such as potassium. Vomiting can cause the esophagus to become inflamed and glands near the cheeks to become swollen. As in anorexia nervosa, bulimia may lead to irregular menstrual periods. Psychological effects include compulsive stealing as well as possible indications of obsessive-compulsive disorder, an illness characterized by repetitive thoughts and behaviors. Obsessive-compulsive disorder can also accompany anorexia nervosa. As with anorexia nervosa, bulimia typically begins during adolescence. Eventually, half of those with anorexia nervosa will develop bulimia. The condition occurs most often in women but is also found in men.

Binge-eating disorder is found in about two percent of the general population. As many as one-third of this group are men. It also affects older women, though with less frequency. Recent research shows that binge-eating disorder occurs in about 30 percent of people participating in medically supervised weight control programs. This disorder differs from bulimia because its sufferers do not purge. Individuals with binge-eating disorder feel that they lose control of themselves when eating. They eat large quantities of food and do not stop until they are uncomfortably full. Most sufferers are overweight or obese and have a history of weight fluctuations. As a result, they are prone to the serious medical problems associated with obesity, such as high cholesterol, high blood pressure, and diabetes. Obese individuals also have a higher risk for gallbladder disease, heart disease, and some types of cancer. Usually they have more difficulty losing weight and keeping it off than do people with other serious weight problems. Like anorexic and bulimic sufferers who exhibit psychological problems, individuals with binge-eating disorder have high rates of simultaneously occurring psychiatric illnesses—especially depression.

369. Fatalities occur in what percent of people with anorexia nervosa?
a. two
b. ten
c. fifteen
d. thirty

370. Which of the following consequences do all the eating disorders mentioned in the passage have in common?
a. heart ailments
b. stomach rupture
c. swollen joints
d. diabetes

371. According to the passage, people with binge-eating disorder are prone to all of the following EXCEPT
a. loss of control
b. depression
c. low blood pressure
d. high cholesterol

372. Based on the information in the passage, which of the following is NOT a true statement about people with eating disorders?
a. People with anorexia nervosa commonly have a blood-related deficiency.
b. People with anorexia nervosa perceive themselves as overweight.
c. The female population is the primary group affected by eating disorders.
d. Fifty percent of people with bulimia have had anorexia nervosa.

373. People who have an eating disorder but nevertheless appear to be of normal weight are most likely to have
a. obsessive-compulsive disorder
b. bulimia nervosa
c. binge-eating disorder
d. anorexia nervosa

374. Glandular functions of eating disorder patients slow down as a result of
a. lowering body temperatures
b. excessive thirst and urination
c. protective measures taken by the body
d. the loss of essential minerals

375. The inability to eliminate body waste is related to
a. dehydration
b. an inflamed esophagus
c. the abuse of laxatives
d. weight control programs

376. According to the passage, which of the following is true of bulimia patients?

a. They may demonstrate unpredictable social behavior.
b. They often engage in compulsive exercise.
c. They are less susceptible to dehydration than are anorexia patients.
d. They frequently experience stomach ruptures.

377. Which of the following represent up to two-thirds of the binge-eating disorder population?

a. older males
b. older females
c. younger males
d. younger females.

SET 53 (Answers begin on page 169.)

The next few sets of passages are law-enforcement-related and objective. Some of the questions are review questions. Some ask you to make simple inferences and to think about the purpose of the passage and its intended audience. Even in objective writing, you can pick up something of the author's attitude toward the subject. For example, the first passage in this set discusses a police department policy that some officers follow reluctantly. Consider the underlined word "cronyism." How would the effect of the sentence have been different if the author had chosen a more positive word?

In many police departments, detectives who want to be promoted further must first spend an extended period of time working in the internal affairs division. Not only do these officers become thoroughly versed in detecting police misconduct, they also become familiar with the circumstances and attitudes out of which such conduct might arise. Placement in internal affairs reduces the possibility that a commanding officer might be too lenient in investigating or disciplining a colleague. The transfer to internal affairs also separates a detective from his or her precinct, reducing the prospect of cronyism, and it familiarizes the detective with serving in a supervisorial capacity.

378. According to the passage, detectives are transferred to internal affairs in order to
   a. enable them to identify situations which might lead to police misconduct
   b. familiarize them with the laws regarding police misconduct
   c. ensure that they are closely supervised
   d. increase the staff of the internal affairs division

379. Who, according to the passage, must spend an extended period working for the internal affairs department?
   a. detectives interested in police misconduct
   b. all detectives
   c. detectives interested in advancement
   d. officers who want to become detectives

380. The internal affairs requirement is apparently intended to
   a. teach detectives how to conduct their own police work properly
   b. demonstrate to the community that the police department takes internal affairs seriously
   c. strengthen the internal affairs division
   d. make supervisors more effective in preventing police misconduct

381. As used in the passage, the underlined word cronyism implies
   a. sticking up for one's partner even if it means covering up wrongdoing
   b. being a friend to one's partner in good times and bad
   c. being loyal to one's partner, even if it means putting oneself in danger
   d. defending one's' partner even when that partner's work is substandard

In order for our society to make decisions about the kinds of punishments we will impose on convicted criminals, we must understand why we punish criminals. Some people argue that retribution is the purpose of punishment and that, therefore, the punishment must in some direct way fit the crime. This view is based on the belief that a person who commits a crime deserves to be punished. Because the punishment must fit the specific crime, the theory of retribution allows a sentencing judge to consider the circumstances of each crime, criminal, and victim in imposing a sentence.

Another view, the deterrence theory, promotes punishment in order to discourage commission of future crimes. In this view, punishment need not relate directly to the crime committed, because the point is to deter both a specific criminal and the general public from committing crimes in the future. However, punishment must necessarily be uniform and consistently applied, in order for the members of the public to understand how they would be punished if they committed a crime. Laws setting sentencing guidelines are based on the deterrence theory and do not allow a judge to consider the specifics of a particular crime in sentencing a convicted criminal.

382. According to the passage, punishment
- a. is rarely an effective deterrent to future crimes
- b. must fit the crime in question
- c. may be imposed for differing reasons
- d. is imposed solely at the discretion of a judge

383. The retribution theory of punishment
- a. is no longer considered valid
- b. holds that punishment must fit the crime committed
- c. applies only to violent crimes
- d. allows a jury to recommend the sentence that should be imposed

384. The passage suggests that a person who believes that the death penalty results in fewer murders most likely also believes in
- a. the deterrence theory
- b. the retribution theory
- c. giving judges considerable discretion in imposing sentences
- d. the integrity of the criminal justice system

385. A person who believes in the deterrence theory would probably also support
- a. non-unanimous jury verdicts
- b. early release of prisoners because of prison overcrowding
- c. a broad definition of the insanity defense
- d. allowing television broadcasts of court proceedings

386. The theories described in the passage differ in
- a. the amount of leeway they would allow judges in determining sentences
- b. the number of law enforcement professionals who espouse them
- c. their concern for the rights of the accused
- d. their concern for protecting society from crime

SET 54 (Answers begin on page 170.)

Consider the following passage whose subject might affect anyone. Think about the author's purpose in writing the passage (to inform? to warn? to simply describe a situation?). How might the author have discussed the subject in a different way so that it would have had a different effect? Suppose the author had considered the stalking law to be a poor idea?

Stalking—the "willful, malicious, and repeated following and harassing of another person"—is probably as old as human society. But in the United States, until 1990, no substantive law existed to protect the stalking victim. The most that police officials could do was arrest the stalker for a minor offense or suggest the victim obtain a restraining order, a civil remedy often ignored by the offender. (One of the Orange County victims mentioned below was shot by her husband while carrying a restraining order in her purse.) Frightened victims had their worst fears confirmed: They would have to be harmed—or killed—before anything could be done

In 1990, however, partly because of the 1989 stalker-murder of television star Rebecca Schaeffer, and partly because of the 1990 stalker-murders of four Orange County women in a single six-week period, California drafted the first anti-stalking law. Now most states have similar laws.

The solution is not perfect: Some stalkers are too mentally deranged or obsessed to fear a prison term. There is danger, however small, of abuse of the law, particularly in marital disputes. Most importantly, both police and society need better education about stalking, especially about its often sexist underpinnings. (The majority of stalking victims are women terrorized by former husbands or lovers.)

But the laws are a start, carrying with them felony penalties of up to ten years in prison for those who would attempt to control or possess others through intimidation and terror.

387. Which of the following best expresses the main idea of the passage?

a. More education is needed about sexism, as it is the most important element in the crime of stalking.
b. Stalking is thought of as a new kind of crime, but has probably existed throughout human history.
c. The new anti-stalking legislation is an important weapon against the crime of stalking, though it is not the complete answer.
d. Today almost every state in the U.S. has an effective, if not perfect, anti-stalking law.

388. Based on the passage, which of the following is likely the most common question asked of police by stalking victims prior to 1990?

a. How can I get a restraining order?
b. Does he have to hurt me before you'll arrest him?
c. Why is this person stalking me?
d. Is it legal for me to carry a weapon in my purse?

389. Which of the following is NOT mentioned in the passage as a weakness in the new anti-stalking legislation?

a. The laws alone might not deter some stalkers.
b. A person might be wrongly accused of being a stalker.
c. Neither the police nor the public completely understand the crime.
d. Victims do not yet have adequate knowledge about anti-stalking laws.

390. Based on the passage, which of the following is the main reason restraining orders are ineffective in preventing stalking?

a. No criminal charges can be leveled against the violator.
b. Most stalkers are mentally deranged.
c. Law enforcement officials do not take such orders seriously.
d. Restraining orders apply only to married couples.

391. Based on the information in the passage, which of the following did the murders of Rebecca Schaeffer and the Orange County woman mentioned in the first paragraph have in common?

a. Both murders provided impetus for anti-stalking laws.
b. Both victims sought, but could not obtain, legal protection.
c. Both victims were stalked and killed by a husband or lover.
d. Both murders were the result of sexism.

392. Which of the following is NOT a stated or implied motive for stalking?

a. to own the victim
b. to terrify the victim
c. to rob the victim
d. to badger the victim

SET 55 (Answers begin on page 170.)

Consider the unpleasant information in the next passage. What if the author had sensationalized this subject, as is often done on TV? How might the word choices have been different? Or suppose the author had simply boiled the passage down to objective statistics? How would the effect have been different in that case?

Most criminals do not suffer from anti-social personality disorder; however, nearly all persons with this disorder have been in trouble with the law. Sometimes labeled "sociopaths," they are a grim problem for society. Their crimes range from con games to murder, and they are set apart by what appears to be a complete lack of conscience. Often attractive and charming, and always inordinately self-confident, they nevertheless demonstrate a disturbing emotional shallowness, as if they had been born without a faculty as vital as sight or hearing. These individuals are not legally insane, nor do they suffer from the distortions of thought associated with mental illness; however, some experts believe they are mentally ill. If so, it is an illness that is exceptionally resistant to treatment, particularly since these individuals have a marked inability to learn from the past. It is this latter trait that makes them a special problem for law enforcement officials. Their ability to mimic true emotion enables them to convince prison officials, judges, and psychiatrists that they feel remorse. When released from incarceration, however, they go back to their old tricks, to their con games, their impulsive destructiveness, and their sometimes lethal deceptions.

393. Based on the passage, which of the following is likely NOT a characteristic of the person with anti-social personality disorder?

a. delusions of persecution
b. feelings of superiority
c. inability to suffer deeply
d. inability to feel joy

394. Which of the following careers would probably best suit the person with anti-social personality?

a. soldier with ambition to make officer
b. warden of a large penitentiary
c. loan officer in a bank
d. salesperson dealing in non-existent real estate

395. Based on the passage, which of the following words best sums up the inner emotional life of the person with anti-social personality?

a. angry
b. empty
c. anxious
d. repressed

396. According to the passage, which of the following characteristics is most helpful to the person with anti-social personality in getting out of trouble with the law?

a. inability to learn from the past
b. ability to mimic the emotions of others
c. attractiveness and charm
d. indifference to the suffering of others

SET 56 (Answers begin on page 170.)

These sets of general-interest passages are not necessarily more difficult than the ones you've already covered—in fact some are actually simpler than the science-related passages you read earlier. However, they do call more heavily for the special skill of making inferences, of identifying ideas that are not explicitly stated in the text.

In the summer, the northern hemisphere is slanted toward the sun, making the days longer and warmer than in winter. The first day of summer, June 21, is called summer solstice and is also the longest day of the year. However, June 21 marks the beginning of winter in the southern hemisphere, when that hemisphere is tilted away from the sun.

397. According to the passage, when it is summer in the northern hemisphere, in the southern hemisphere it is

a. spring
b. summer
c. autumn
d. winter

398. It can be inferred from the passage that, in the southern hemisphere, June twenty-first is

a. autumnal equinox
b. winter solstice
c. vernal equinox
d. summer solstice

Jessie Street is sometimes called the Australian Eleanor Roosevelt. Like Roosevelt, Street lived a life of privilege, while at the same time devoting her efforts to working for the rights of the disenfranchised, including workers, women, refugees, and Aborigines. In addition, she gained international fame when she was the only woman on the Australian delegation to the conference that founded the United Nations — just as Eleanor Roosevelt was for the United States.

399. Which of the following inferences may be drawn from the information presented in the passage?

a. Eleanor Roosevelt and Jessie Street worked together to include women in the United Nations Charter.
b. Usually, people who live lives of privilege do not spend much time participating in political activities.
c. Discrimination in Australia is much worse than it ever was in the United States.
d. At the time of the formation of the United Nations, few women were involved in international affairs.

Light pollution is a growing problem worldwide. Like other forms of pollution, light pollution degrades the quality of the environment. Where once it was possible to look up at the night sky and see thousands of twinkling stars in the inky blackness, one now sees little more than the yellow glare of urban sky glow. When we lose the ability to connect visually with the vastness of the universe by looking up at the night sky, we lose our connection with something profoundly important to the human spirit, our sense of wonder.

400. The passage implies that the most serious damage done by light pollution is to our

a. artistic appreciation
b. sense of physical well-being
c. cultural advancement
d. spiritual selves

Deep in the sandstone about eighteen kilometers from Aldershott Prison on the eastern side of Botany Bay, there was a seam of coal. What better form of extra punishment than to turn the convicts into miners, condemned to hard labor deep underground in darkness, with the immediate, ever-present threat of ________.

401. Which word or phrase makes the most sense in the context?

a. black lung
b. cruel foremen
c. re-arrest
d. cave-ins

SET 57 (Answers begin on page 171.)

Here are more short passages that ask you to make simple inferences, to identify *implicit*, as opposed to explicit, ideas.

Moscow has a history of chaotic periods of war that ended with the destruction of a once largely wooden city and the building of a "new" city on top of the rubble of the old. The result is a layered city, with each tier holding information about a part of Russia's past. In some areas of the city, archaeologists have reached the layer from 1147, the year of Moscow's founding. Among the findings from the various periods of Moscow's history are carved bones, metal tools, pottery, glass, jewelry, and crosses.

402. From the passage, the reader can infer that
 a. the people of Moscow are more interested in modernization than in preservation
 b. the Soviet government destroyed many of the historic buildings in Russia
 c. Moscow is the oldest large city in Russia, founded in 1147
 d. Moscow has a history of invasions, with each new conqueror razing past structures

Originating in the 1920s, the Pyramid scheme is one of the oldest con games going. Honest people are often pulled in, thinking the scheme is a legitimate investment enterprise. The first customer to "fall for" the Pyramid scheme will actually make big money and will therefore persuade friends and relatives to join also. The chain then continues with the con artist who originated the scheme pocketing, rather than investing, the money. Finally the pyramid collapses, but by that time the scam artist will usually have moved out of town, leaving no forwarding address.

403. This paragraph implies that
 a. the first customer of a Pyramid scheme is the most gullible
 b. the con artist who sets up a Pyramid scheme must have a modicum of patience
 c. the Pyramid scheme had its heyday in the 1920s
 d. the Pyramid scheme got its name from its structure

The motives for skyjacking are as various as the people who commit the crime. Motives may be political or personal, or there may appear to be no motive at all. Skyjackers range from well-organized groups of terrorists to lonely individuals who are mentally ill, from highly educated persons to those who are nearly illiterate, from atheists to religious fanatics. This crime is one of the most unpredictable because it is so difficult for law enforcement officials to create an accurate profile of a skyjacker.

404. The reader can infer from the paragraph that
 a. people who commit skyjackings are unpredictable
 b. only someone who is emotionally off-balance would commit a skyjacking
 c. skyjackers are either highly educated or nearly illiterate
 d. creating a criminal profile depends on the perpetrators having traits in common

SET 58 (Answers begin on page 171.)

In reading these next passages, think particularly about the writer's purpose and intended audience. Ask yourself, Is the piece meant to entertain? Inform? Persuade?

Authentic Dhurrie rugs are hand-woven in India. Today, they are usually made of wool, but they are descendants of cotton floor- and bed-coverings. In fact, the name Dhurrie comes from the Indian word *dari*, which means threads of cotton. The rugs are noted for their soft colors and their varieties of design and make a stunning focal point for any living room or dining room.

405. Which of the following is the most likely intended audience for the passage?

a. people studying traditional Indian culture
b. people who are studying Indian domestic customs
c. people learning to operate a rug loom
d. people who enjoy interior decorating

Over the last twenty years, worldwide illiteracy rates have consistently declined. The main reason for this decline is the sharp increase of literacy rates among young women, which is the result of campaigns to increase educational opportunities for girls. For example, between 1970 and 1990, the literacy rate among women in the United Arab Emirates increased from seven percent to 76 percent.

406. Based on the passage, the author would tend to agree with which of the following statements?

a. Men and women should have equal access to education.
b. It has been shown that women with increased education have fewer children.
c. Males traditionally have a greater need for higher education.
d. Throughout the world, women need medical care more than the ability to read.

Emperor Charlemagne of the Franks was crowned in 800 A.D. The Frankish Empire at that time extended over what is now Germany, Italy, and France. Charlemagne died in 814, but his brief reign marked the dawn of a distinctly European culture. The artists and thinkers that helped create this European civilization drew on the ancient texts of the Germanic, Celtic, Greek, Roman, Hebrew, and Christian worlds. ______________________. These mores in turn laid the groundwork for the laws, customs, and even attitudes of today's Europeans.

407. According to the passage, for how many years was Charlemagne Emperor of the Franks?
a. fourteen years
b. fifteen years
c. thirteen years
d. sixteen years

408. Which of the following is the best meaning of the word *culture* as it is used in the passage?
a. the fashionable class
b. a community of inter-related individuals
c. a partnership
d. an organized group with a common goal

409. Which sentence, if inserted into the blank line in the passage, would be most consistent with the writer's purpose and intended audience?
a. Cultural traditions function to identify members of a culture to one another and, also, to allow the individual to self-identify.
b. Many of the traditions of these cultures remained active in Frankish society for centuries.
c. When tradition is lacking or is not honored by the younger generation in a society, there is danger that the culture will be lost.
d. I don't think it is necessary to discuss the origin of these traditions; it will only muddy the water.

SET 59 (Answers begin on page 171.)

Once again, think about the author's intended audience and purpose for writing these next passages. What clues can you pick up from the writing style about the author's attitude toward the subject? Is the attitude positive? Negative? Objective?

It has been more than twenty-five years since the National Aeronautic and Space Administration (NASA) last sent a craft to land on the moon. The Lunar Prospector took off in January of 1998, in the first moon shot since astronauts last walked on the moon in 1972. This time, the moon-traveler is only a low-cost robot, who will spend a year on the surface of the moon, collecting minerals and ice.

Unlike the moon shots of the 1960s and 1970s, Lunar Prospector does not carry a camera, so the American public will not get to see new pictures of the moon's surface. ______________________________ ___________. Scientists are anxious for the results of one exploration in particular—that done by the neutron spectrometer. Using this instrument, Prospector will examine the moon's poles, searching for signs of water ice. There has long been speculation that frozen water from comets may have accumulated in craters at one of the moon's poles and may still be there, as this pole is permanently shielded from the sun. The neutron spectrometer seeks out the hydrogen atoms in water and can detect the presence of as little as one cup of water in a cubic yard of soil.

410. Which sentence, if inserted into the blank line in the second paragraph, would be most consistent with the writer's purpose and intended audience?

a. You won't, therefore, be able to see if the surface of the moon has changed much in thirty years.
b. Instead, Prospector carries instruments that will map the make-up of the entire surface of the moon.
c. I don't believe that new pictures would prove very interesting, anyway.
d. However, the topography of the lunar terrain retains a mundane familiarity that is not consistent with the nature of NASA's *raison d'etre* and will contribute little to advancements *vis a vis* missions such as Sojourner.

411. Which of the following is the best meaning of the underlined word speculation as it is used in the second paragraph of the passage?

a. a theory
b. an investment
c. a vision
d. an image

412. Which of the following kinds of publications would most likely contain this passage?

a. an astrophysics text book
b. a history text book
c. a collection of personal essays
d. a general circulation magazine

In 1899, Czar Nicholas II of Russia, invited the nations of the world to a conference at The Hague. This conference—and a follow-up organized by Theodore Roosevelt in 1907—ushered in a period of vigorous growth in international law. This growth was in response to several factors, not least of which was the increasing potential for destruction of modern warfare. The recently concluded Civil War in the United States made this potential clear.

During this growth, the subjects of international law were almost exclusively restricted to the relationships that countries had with one another. Issues of trade and warfare dominated both the disputes and the agreements of the period. ________, the developments of this period paved the way for further expansion of international law, which has occurred in the last several years. ________, organizations such as the United Nations and the International Court of Justice are greatly concerned not only with the way countries deal with one another, but the ways in which they treat their own citizens.

413. Which words or phrases, if inserted in order into the blanks in the passage, would help the reader understand the sequence of the author's ideas?

a. Therefore; In addition
b. However; Now
c. Furthermore; Yet
d. Even if; On the other hand

414. According to the passage, what was the impact of the U.S. Civil War on the development of international law?

a. It allowed armaments manufacturers to test new weapons.
b. It diminished the influence of the United States internationally.
c. It resulted in the suspension of agriculture exports from Southern states.
d. It highlighted the increasing destructive capabilities of modern warfare.

415. Which of the following is the best meaning of the underlined phrase ushered in as it is used in the passage?

a. escorted
b. progressed
c. guarded
d. heralded

SET 60 (Answers begin on page 172.)

Here's a somewhat light but informational passage. Think about how the writer's tone, style, and word choice differ from those in some of the more serious passages you've read. Don't forget to practice other techniques you've learned about reading. Remember to look at the unfamiliar words in terms of their context.

(1) Milton Hershey was born near the small village of Derry Church, Pennsylvania, in 1857. It was a __________ beginning that did not foretell his later popularity. Milton only attended school through the fourth grade; at that point, he was apprenticed to a printer in a nearby town. Fortunately for all chocolate lovers, Milton did not excel as a printer. After a while, he left the printing business and was apprenticed to a Lancaster, Pennsylvania candy maker. It was apparent he had found his calling in life and, at the age of eighteen, he opened his own candy store in Philadelphia. In spite of his talents as a candy maker, the shop failed after six years.

(2) It may come as a surprise to Milton Hershey's fans today that his first candy success came with the manufacture of caramel. After the failure of his Philadelphia store, Milton headed for Denver, where he learned the art of making caramels. There he took a job with a local manufacturer who insisted on using fresh milk in making his caramels; Milton saw that this made the caramels especially tasty. After a time in Denver, Milton once again attempted to open his own candy-making businesses, in Chicago, New Orleans, and New York City. Finally, in 1886, he went to Lancaster, Pennsylvania, where he raised the money necessary to try again. This company—the Lancaster Caramel Company—made Milton's reputation as a master candy maker.

(3) In 1893, Milton attended the Chicago International Exposition, where he saw a display of German chocolate-making implements. Captivated by the equipment, he purchased it for his Lancaster candy factory and began producing chocolate, which he used for coating his caramels. By the next year, production had grown to include cocoa, sweet chocolate, and baking chocolate. The Hershey Chocolate company was born in 1894 as a <u>subsidiary</u> of the Lancaster Caramel Company. Six years later, Milton sold the caramel company, but retained the rights, and the equipment, to make chocolate. He believed that a large market of chocolate consumers was waiting for someone to produce reasonably priced candy. He was right.

(4) Milton Hershey returned to the village where he had been born, in the heart of dairy country and opened his chocolate manufacturing plant. With access to all the fresh milk he needed, he began producing the finest milk chocolate. The plant that opened in a small Pennsylvania village in 1905 is today the largest chocolate factory in the world. The confections created at this facility are favorites in the U.S. and internationally.

(5) The area where the factory is located is now known as Hershey, Pennsylvania. Within the first decades of its existence, the town of Hershey thrived, as did the chocolate business. A bank, a school, churches, a department store, even a park and a trolley system all appeared in short order; the town soon even had a zoo. Today, a visit to the area reveals the Hershey Medical Center, Milton Hershey School, and Hershey's Chocolate World, a theme park where visitors are greeted by a giant Reeses Peanut Butter Cup. All of these things—and a huge number of happy chocolate lovers—were made possible because a caramel maker visited the Chicago Exposition of 1893!

416. According to information contained in the passage, the reader can infer which of the following?

a. Chocolate is popular in every country in the world.
b. Reeses Peanut Butter Cups are manufactured by the Hershey Chocolate Company.
c. Chocolate had never been manufactured in the U.S. before Milton Hershey did it.
d. The Hershey Chocolate Company now makes more money from Hershey's Chocolate World than from the manufacture and sale of chocolate.

417. Which of the following best defines the word subsidiary as used in paragraph three?

a. a company owned entirely by one person
b. a company founded to support another company
c. a company that is not incorporated
d. a company controlled by another company

418. The writer's main purpose in this passage is to

a. recount the founding of the Hershey Chocolate Company
b. describe the process of manufacturing chocolate
c. compare the popularity of chocolate to other candies
d. explain how apprenticeships work

419. According to the passage, Milton Hershey sold his caramel company in

a. 1894
b. 1900
c. 1904
d. 1905

420. The mentions of the Chicago International Exposition of 1893 in the passage indicate that

a. the exposition in Chicago is held once every three years
b. the theme of the exposition of 1893 was "Food from Around the World"
c. the exposition contained displays from a variety of countries
d. the site of the exposition is now a branch of the Hershey Chocolate Company

421. Which of the following words best fits in the blank in paragraph one of the passage?

a. dramatic
b. modest
c. undignified
d. rewarding

SET 61 (Answers begin on page 173.)

Again, think about the author's purpose in writing the passages in this next set. What is the author's attitude toward the subject? Are there implicit ideas or only explicit ones?

A healthy diet with proper nutrition is essential for maintaining good overall health. Since vitamins were discovered earlier in this century, people have routinely been taking vitamin supplements for this purpose. The Recommended Dietary Allowance (RDA) is a frequently used nutritional standard for maintaining optimal health. The RDA specifies the recommended amount of a number of nutrients for people in many different age and sex groups. The National Research Council's Committee on Diet and Health has proposed a definition of the RDA to be that amount of a nutrient which meets the needs of 98 percent of the population.

The RDA approach ________________________. First, it is based on the assumption that it is possible to accurately define nutritional requirements for a given group. However, individual nutritional requirements can vary widely within each group. The efficiency with which a person converts food intake into nutrients can also vary widely. Certain foods when eaten in combination actually prevent the absorption of nutrients. For example, spinach combined with milk reduces the amount of calcium available to the body from the milk. Also, the RDA approach specifies a different dietary requirement for each age and sex; however, it is clearly unrealistic to expect a homemaker to prepare a different menu for each family member. Still, although we cannot rely solely upon RDA to ensure our overall long-term health, it can be a useful guide so long as its limitations are recognized.

422. Which of the following would best fit in the blank in the first sentence of paragraph two?

a. is based on studies by respected nutritionists
b. has a number of shortcomings
c. has been debunked in the last few years
d. is full of holes

423. With which of the following would the author most likely agree?

a. The RDA approach should be replaced by a more realistic nutritional guide.
b. The RDA approach should be supplemented with more specific nutritional guides.
c. In spite of its flaws, the RDA approach is definitely the best guide to good nutrition.
d. The RDA approach is most suitable for a large family.

Businesses today routinely keep track of large amounts of both financial and non-financial information. Sales departments keep track of current and potential customers; marketing departments keep track of product details and regional demographics; accounting departments keep track of financial data and issue reports. To be useful, all this data must be organized into a meaningful and useful system. Such a system is called a management information system, abbreviated MIS. The financial hub of the MIS is accounting.

Accounting is the information system that records, analyzes, and reports economic transactions, enabling decision-makers to make informed choices when allocating scarce economic resources. It is a tool that enables the user, whether a business entity or an individual, to make wiser, more informed economic choices. It is an aid to planning, controlling, and evaluating a broad range of activities. A financial accounting system is intended for use by both the management of an organization and those outside the organization. Because it is important that financial accounting reports be interpreted correctly, financial accounting is subject to a set of ___________ guidelines called "generally accepted accounting principles" (GAAP).

424. This passage is most likely taken from
a. a newspaper column
b. a business textbook
c. an essay about modern business
d. a government document

425. The word that would fit most correctly into the blank in the final sentence is
a. discretionary
b. convenient
c. austere
d. stringent

426. According to the information in the passage, which of the following is LEAST likely to be a function of accounting?
a. helping businesspeople make sound judgments
b. assisting with the marketing of products
c. producing reports of many different kinds of transactions
d. assisting companies in important planning activities

20 Academy Street, P.O. Box 7100, Norwalk, CT 06852-9879

TEN TIPS TO PASSING ANY TEST

To provide you with the test prep and career information you need, we would appreciate your help. Please answer the following questions and return this postage paid survey. As our Thank You, we will send you our "Ten Tips To Passing Any Test"—surefire ways to score your best on classroom and/or job-related exams.

Name: ______________________

Address: ______________________

____

Age: __________ Sex: ❒ Male ❒ Female

Highest Level of School Completed: ❒ High School ❒ College

1) I am currently:
   A student—Year/level: ______________
   Employed—Job title: ______________
   Other—Please explain: ______________

2) Title of the book this card came from:

____

3) Jobs/careers of interest to me are:
   1. ______________________
   2. ______________________
   3. ______________________

4) If you are a student, did your guidance/career counselor provide you with job information/materials? ____
   Name & Location of School: ______________

____

____

5) What newspapers and/or magazines do you subscribe to or read regularly? ______________

____

6) Do you own a computer? ______________
   Do you have Internet access? ______________
   How often do you go on-line? ______________

7) The last time you visited a bookstore, did you make a purchase? ______________
   Have you purchased career-related materials from bookstores? ______________

8) Which radio stations do you listen to regularly (please give call letters and city name)?

____

____

9) Do you subscribe to Cable TV? ______________

10) How did you hear about this LearningExpress book?
   An ad? ______________
   An order form in the back of another book? ______
   A recommendation? ______________
   A bookstore? ______________
   Other? ______________

11) Please check (or rank) your reasons for purchasing this book:

Content ____________ Price ____________

Recommended to you ____ Only book available ____

LearningExpress books are also available in the test prep/study guide section of your local bookstore.

NO POSTAGE
NECESSARY
IF MAILED
IN THE
UNITED STATES

BUSINESS REPLY MAIL

FIRST CLASS MAIL PERMIT NO. 150 NORWALK, CT

LearningExpress
20 Academy Street
P.O. Box 7100
Norwalk, CT 06852-9879

LearningExpress

The new leader in test preparation and career guidance!

LearningExpress is an affiliate of Random House, Inc.

SET 62 (Answers begin on page 173.)

Look for clues to the author's audience and purpose in the subject matter, style, and tone of the passages. Is the style formal or informal? Is the tone light or heavy? Is the author's attitude objective or subjective or a little of both?

Typically people think of genius, whether it manifests in Mozart's composing symphonies at age five or Einstein's discovery of relativity, as having a quality not just of the supernatural, but also of the eccentric. People see genius as a "good" abnormality; moreover, they think of genius as a completely unpredictable abnormality. Until recently, psychologists regarded the quirks of genius as too erratic to describe intelligibly; however, Anna Findley's ground-breaking study uncovers predictable patterns in the biographies of geniuses. These patterns do not dispel the common belief that there is a kind of supernatural intervention in the lives of unusually talented men and women, however, even though they occur with regularity. __________, Findley shows that all geniuses experience three intensely productive periods in their lives, one of which always occurs shortly before their deaths; this is true whether the genius lives to nineteen or ninety.

427. Which word or phrase, if inserted into the blank space above, best defines the relationship of the last sentence in the passage to the one preceding it?
a. For example
b. Despite this
c. However
d. In other words

428. According to the information presented in the passage, what is the general populace's opinion of genius?
a. It is predictable and uncommon.
b. It is supercilious and abnormal.
c. It is unpredictable and erratic.
d. It is extraordinary and erratic.

429. Which of the following would be the best title for passage?
a. Understanding Mozarts and Einsteins
b. Predicting the Life of a Genius
c. The Uncanny Patterns in the Lives of Geniuses
d. Pattern and Disorder in the Lives of Geniuses

430. Given the information in the passage, which of the following statements is true?
a. Anna Findley is a biographer.
b. All geniuses are eccentric and unpredictable.
c. A genius has three prolific times in his or her life.
d. Mozart discovered relativity.

SET 63 (Answers begin on page 173.)

What is the author's purpose in writing the passage in this set? Is it to persuade or merely inform? How does the author feel about the subject, positive or negative?

The word *vodoun* is believed to have come from the West African country of Benin—at one time called Dahomey. The Dahomey word *vodu*, means "gods" and at some point in history was transformed into the word "voodoo" which is now considered a pejorative. The etymology of the word lends credence to the idea that *vodoun* is best understood as a revision of various African religious beliefs. In spite of this African foundation, however, *vodoun* is best known in its western hemisphere incarnation as the national religion of Haiti. In the United States, the practice of *vodoun* is protected under freedom of religion principles, although some communities have occasionally tried to outlaw the practice of certain of its rites. With an essential basis in spiritualism, the most common ceremonies of *vodoun* feature priests and priestesses who become conduits for spirits which are asked to protect devotees and to assist the priests or priestesses in foretelling the future.

Vodoun is sometimes described, by those unfamiliar with it, as superstition, but it is not. Superstition is the belief in things that are known, or commonly believed to be, untrue. (There is no scientific evidence, for example, that breaking a mirror will result in seven years of bad luck. To believe that it will, then, is superstitious.) However, although most mainstream religions in the United States now are monotheistic, most of them do ask practitioners to believe in a god who can intercede in human interactions and protect believers from harm. This is no different from the beliefs of *vodoun* practitioners.

431. The writer's main purpose in writing this selection is to
- a. describe the rites involved in the religion of *vodoun*
- b. argue that *vodoun* is, in some senses, a superstition
- c. persuade readers that *vodoun* is a valid religion
- d. explain the etymology of the word *vodoun*

432. Which of the following best defines the word etymology as it is used in the first paragraph of the selection?
- a. the science of defining words
- b. the science of uncovering the origin of words
- c. the science of explaining the symbolism of words
- d. the science of word construction

433. Which of the following statements from the selection indicate the writer's opinion, rather than fact?
- a. *Vodoun* is the national religion of Haiti.
- b. In the United States, some communities have occasionally tried to outlaw the practice of certain *vodoun* rites.
- c. The belief in mainstream religions that a god can intercede in human affairs is no different from the beliefs of *vodoun* practitioners.
- d. The word "*vodoun*" is believed to have come from the West African country of Benin—at one time called Dahomey.

434. Which of the following is a valid conclusion based on the passage?

a. *Vodoun,* like most mainstream religions, is a monotheistic belief system.
b. *Vodoun* is based on beliefs that are proven falsehoods.
c. *Vodoun* is only practiced in Haiti.
d. *Vodoun* worshippers have encountered prejudice in their communities.

435. Which of the following details is used in the passage to support the writer's contention that *vodoun* is similar to mainstream religions?

a. Like mainstream religions in the United States, *vodoun* utilizes priests and priestesses.
b. Mainstream religions believe in an afterlife just as *vodoun* does.
c. *Vodoun* has rites and rituals.
d. Mainstream religions believe in divine intervention.

SET 64 (Answers begin on page 174.)

Perhaps you love to read literature. Perhaps you like the classics, thrillers, *and* historical fiction. Or perhaps you are intimidated by literature because you remember a teacher asking, "What's the theme of this piece?" or "What does the symbolism *mean*?" and you had no idea. After progressing through this book, you are better armed for these questions. Approach this relatively simple set as you would a non-fiction piece. Ask, "What is the main idea?" (This is nearly the same as asking, "What is the theme?") Ask, "What is this piece really about?"

As soon as she sat down on the airplane, Rachel almost began to regret telling the travel agent that she wanted an exotic and romantic vacation. As the plane hurled toward Rio de Janeiro, she read the information on Carnival that was in the pocket of the seat in front of hers. The very definition of Carnival made her shiver—"from the Latin *carnavale*, meaning a farewell to the flesh." She was searching for excitement, but had no intention of bidding her skin good-bye. Carnival, the brochure informed her, originated in Europe in the Middle Ages and served as a break from the requirements of daily life and society. Most of all, it allowed the hard-working and desperately poor serfs the opportunity to ridicule their wealthy and normally humorless masters. Rachel, a middle manager in a computer firm, wasn't entirely sure whether she was more serf or master. Should she be making fun, or would others be mocking her? She was strangely relieved when the plane landed, as though her fate were decided.

Rachel chewed on her lower lip as she stood before the mirror in her hotel room, choosing first one dress then another, trying to decide which outfit was the most serf-like. Nothing in her "dress for success" seminar had prepared her for this all-important decision. Finally, wearing her brightest blouse and skirt, she headed for the street, determined to find adventure.

436. What is this passage mainly about?
a. what life is like in Rio de Janeiro
b. the history of Carnival
c. a traveler on an exciting vacation
d. how to dress for success

437. Rachel was nervous on the airplane because she
a. was afraid to fly
b. thought Carnival sounded very exotic
c. forgot her traveler's checks
d. was worried she would lose her luggage

438. The passage implies that Rachel
a. is traveling alone
b. takes a vacation every year
c. has never traveled abroad before
d. speaks Portuguese

439. Rachel seems to be a person who
  a. does not usually travel
  b. is dissatisfied with her life
  c. works too hard
  d. is interested in trying new things

440. According to the passage, Carnival
  a. lasts for several days
  b. originated in Europe
  c. occurs in February
  d. is famous for good food

441. Which of these sentences would most logically begin the next paragraph of this story?
  a. Settling herself comfortably at a table in the hotel coffee shop, Rachel began writing a post card to her mother.
  b. Later that night, as Rachel tossed in her bed, she wondered whether Bob ever thought about her.
  c. Rachel entered the huge office building and rode the elevator to the twelfth floor, the location of her 9:00 business meeting.
  d. As soon as she left the hotel, Rachel was surrounded by the sights and sounds of Carnival.

SET 65 (Answers begin on page 174.)

Most fiction reveals its ideas and themes implicitly, rather than explicitly. See what inferences you can make from this story excerpt? Consider the main character. What does she want? What is she afraid of? Do you think she is afraid of more than one thing? Even if you are not told directly, there are plenty of clues in style, tone, word choice.

(1) For perhaps the tenth time since the clock struck two, Sylvia crosses to the front-facing window of her apartment, pulls back the blue curtain and looks down at the street. People hurry along the sidewalk; however, although she watches for several long moments, she sees no one enter her building.

(2) She walks back to the center of the high-ceilinged living room, where she stands frowning and twisting a silver bracelet around and around on her wrist. She is an attractive young woman, although perhaps too thin and with a look that is faintly ascetic; her face is narrow and delicate, her fine, light-brown hair caught back by a tortoiseshell comb. She is restless now, because she is being kept waiting. It is nearly two-thirty—a woman named Lola Parrish was to come at two o'clock to look at the apartment.

(3) She considers leaving a note and going out. The woman is late, after all, and besides, Sylvia is certain that Lola Parrish will not be a suitable person with whom to share the apartment. On the phone she had sounded too old, for one thing, her voice oddly flat and as deep as a man's. However, the moment for saying the apartment was no longer available slipped past, and Sylvia found herself agreeing to the two o'clock appointment. If she leaves now, as she has a perfect right to do, she can avoid the awkwardness of turning the woman away.

(4) Looking past the blue curtain, however, she sees the sky is not clear but veiled by a white haze, and the air is oppressively still. She knows that the haze and the stillness and heat are conditions that often precede a summer thunderstorm, one of the abrupt, swiftly descending electrical storms that have terrified her since she was a child. If a storm comes, she wants to be at home in her own place.

(5) She walks back to the center of the room, aware now that the idea of sharing the apartment, never appealing, born of necessity, has actually begun to repel her. Still, she knows she will have to become accustomed to the notion, because her savings are nearly gone and the small trust fund left her by her father exhausted. She has a job, but it does not pay well, and, although she has considered seeking another (perhaps something connected with music—in her childhood she had played the flute and people had said she was gifted), lately she has found herself dragged down by a strange inertia.

(6) Besides, although her job pays poorly, it suits her. She is a typist in a natural history museum, in an office on the top floor, near the aviary. The man for whom she works, one of the curators, is rarely in, so Sylvia has the office to herself. The aviary consists of three enormous rooms, painted white, each with a high vaulted ceiling. The birds themselves, so beautifully mounted they seem alive, are displayed in elaborate dioramas. Behind glass, they perch in trees with leaves of sculpted metal, appear to soar through painted forests, above painted rivers and marshes. Everything is rendered in exquisite detail. And in her office there is a skylight. The location of the office, so near the open sky, suits her, too, because she is mildly claustrophobic.

442. Which of the following adjectives best describes Sylvia's mood as depicted in the story segment?

a. anxious
b. angry
c. meditative
d. serene

443. Based on the tone of the passage and the description of Sylvia at this moment, which of the following is the most likely reason Sylvia's job "suits her"?

a. Her office is tastefully decorated.
b. She is fond of her employer, the museum curator.
c. She is musical and enjoys the singing of birds.
d. She is able to work alone in a space that feels open.

444. When Sylvia looks out her window, the weather appears

a. gloomy
b. ominous
c. spring-like
d. bracing

445. Based on the story segment, which of the following would most likely describe Sylvia's behavior in relationship to other people?

a. distant
b. overbearing
c. dependent
d. malicious

446. Which of the following is most likely the author's purpose in describing in detail the museum where Sylvia works?

a. Everything in it, though beautiful and tasteful, seems frozen or removed from life and reflects some aspect of Sylvia's character.
b. The fact that it is light and airy and filled with beautiful dioramas reflects Sylvia's youth and her wish for something better.
c. Some part of the story, perhaps a love affair between Sylvia and her boss, will probably take place there.
d. The killing and mounting of the beautiful birds will probably play an important part in the story.

SET 66 (Answers begin on page 175.)

Poetry scares some people to death, mainly because they believe that any poem worth its salt has a "hidden meaning" that they won't understand. But that phrase is misleading. A poem usually does express its ideas implicitly, but the meaning is there to be ferreted out if you work hard enough. In the poetry sets that follow you don't really need outside knowledge to answer the questions. You only need to apply what you've learned so far about other kinds of writing: Look at the context and the word choice. Ask youself, What is the main idea? Expect surprising language, and enjoy it.

The following poem is by Alfred, Lord Tennyson. Consider the title of this poem as a guide to meaning.

The Eagle

He clasps the crag with crooked hands;
Close to the sun in lonely lands,
Ringed with the azure world he stands.

The wrinkled sea beneath him crawls;
He watches from his mountain walls,
And like a thunderbolt he falls.

447. Given the tone of the poem, and noting especially the last line, what is the eagle MOST likely doing in the poem?
a. dying of old age
b. hunting prey
c. learning joyfully to fly
d. keeping watch over a nest of young eagles

448. To which of the following do the underlined words azure world most likely refer?
a. a forest
b. the sky
c. the cliff
d. nature

449. In the second stanza, first line, to which of the following does the verb "crawls" refer?
a. waves
b. sunlight on the water
c. the eagle's prey
d. the eagle itself

SET 67 (Answers begin on page 175.)

When approaching a poem, don't start with the assumption that the meaning is totally concealed or impenetrable. Begin by reading closely for the literal meaning. Who is speaking in the poem? (The speaker may not be the poet.) What is that person's attitude toward his or her subject?

This poem, by Emily Dickinson, is a sort of riddle. Depending on your life experiences, the answer may be immediately clear. Or it may very well not be. Like a good detective, look closely for clues in the language.

A Narrow Fellow in the Grass

A narrow fellow in the grass
Occasionally rides;
You may have met him—did you not?
His notice sudden is.
The grass divides as with a comb,
A spotted shaft is seen,
And then it closes at your feet
And opens further on.

He likes a boggy acre,
A floor too cool for corn,
Yet when a boy, and barefoot,
I more than once at noon
Have passed, I thought, a whip-lash
Unbraiding in the sun,
When, stooping to secure it,
It wrinkled, and was gone.

Several of nature's people
I know and they know me;
I feel for them a transport
Of cordiality;
But never met this fellow,
Attended or alone,
Without a tighter breathing
And zero at the bone.

450. Who or what is the "fellow" in this poem?
a. a whip-lash
b. a snake
c. a gust of wind
d. a boy

451. The phrase "Without a tighter breathing / And zero at the bone" most nearly indicates
a. fright
b. cold
c. grief
d. awe

452. The phrase "nature's people" means
a. nature-lovers
b. children
c. animals
d. neighbors

453. The speaker of this poem is most likely
a. an adult woman
b. an adult man
c. Emily Dickinson, the poet
d. a young boy

SET 68 (Answers begin on page 175.)

It's true that poems often have two levels, one literal, one figurative. This poem, also by Emily Dickinson, is full of images from nature. In exploring the second level of meaning, consider the speaker's attitude, revealed especially through surprising, and jarring, word choices.

Apparently with No Surprise

Apparently with no surprise
To any happy flower,
The frost beheads it at its play
In accidental power.

The blond assassin passes on,
The sun proceeds unmoved
To measure off another day
For an approving God.

454. Which of the following most nearly describes the author's attitude toward nature as expressed in this poem?
a. delight
b. dismay
c. indifference
d. reverence

455. What is "the blond assassin" referred to in the poem?
a. the flowers
b. the frost
c. the sun
d. God

456. The poem implies that the attitude of the flowers toward the frost is one of
a. fear
b. horror
c. acceptance
d. reverence

457. The tone of the poem implies that the speaker probably regards God as
a. benevolent
b. just
c. cruel
d. angry

SET 69 (Answers begin on page 176.)

These next passages are mostly philosophical. Remember, though, that no matter how subtle the subject matter, all the information you need is in the passage itself, and what you've learned so far applies. Look for the main idea. For unfamiliar words and concepts, pay close attention to the surrounding context.

James Carruthers' recent essays attempt to redefine arts criticism as a play of critical intelligence that can take place free from the bonds of political partisanship. In Carruthers' view, this play of the mind, working itself free from constraints, is the only ethical approach to the arts.

458. What is the best definition of the word "play" as it is used in the above passage?

a. to act or conduct oneself in a specified way
b. to move or operate freely within a confined space
c. to pretend to be; mimic the activities of
d. to behave carelessly or indifferently

Poet William Blake believed that true religion is revealed through art, not through nature. For Blake, it is through art also that eternity is revealed. One does not have to die to reach eternity; eternity is the moment of vision. It is only through the reordering of sense impression by the creative imagination that we are able, as Blake says in his "Auguries of Innocence," "To see the World in a Grain of Sand/ . . . And Eternity in an hour."

459. Which of the following would best describe what Blake meant by the words "To see the World in a Grain of Sand/ . . . And Eternity in an hour"?

a. a moment of mystical enlightenment
b. conversion to Christianity
c. a moment of artistic inspiration
d. an hallucinatory experience

460. Which of the following defines Blake's view of nature, as described in the passage?

a. the raw stuff of which the world is made but which does not represent ultimate reality
b. the work of God in a state of innocence before it is corrupted by human beings
c. the world made up of base and corrupt material before it is changed by the perception of the artist at the moment of vision
d. the temporal world that will perish, as opposed to the world of artistic vision that will last forever

SET 70 (Answers begin on page 176.)

Never be intimidated by what seems to be a "heavy" meaning in what you read. Call on all the resources you've gathered in answering the questions in this book. For unfamiliar words, look at context, the words or sentences that immediately surround the problematic words. Read once for meaning. Then go back and underline important points. Outline. Make lists.

In Ralph Waldo Emerson's view, although individual consciousness will eventually be lost, every living thing is part of the blessed Unity, part of the transcendent "over-soul" which is the universe. And so, in the main body of his philosophy, Emerson accepts the indifference of Nature to the individual life, and does not struggle against it. His acceptance of Nature as tending toward overall unity and good in spite of her indifference to the individual is curiously and ironically akin to the Puritan acceptance of the doctrine of Divine Election. In his "Personal Narrative" Jonathan Edwards writes that he finally has "a delightful conviction" of the doctrine of God's sovereignty, of God's choosing according to His divine and arbitrary will, "whom he would to eternal life, and rejecting whom he pleased . . . ." He writes that the doctrine had formerly seemed to him; however, it had finally come to seem "exceedingly pleasant, bright, and sweet." In "Fate," Emerson writes that "Nature will not mind drowning a man or a woman, but swallows your ship like a grain of dust," but that "the central intention of Nature [is] harmony and joy. Let us build altars to the Beautiful Necessity. . . ."

461. Which of the following statements would LEAST effectively support the view of both Emerson and Edwards toward the nature of the universe?
a. God notices the fall of a sparrow.
b. God is all-powerful and all-wise.
c. The universe is a harmonious place.
d. Nature is beautiful and good.

462. Which of the following best describes the main idea of the passage?
a. As philosophers reflecting on the nature of the universe, Ralph Waldo Emerson and Jonathan Edwards are ironically akin to one another.
b. Ralph Waldo Emerson's acceptance of Nature's indifference to the individual is ironically similar to Jonathan Edwards' acceptance of the doctrine of Divine Election.
c. Ralph Waldo Emerson believes in a world ruled by the transcendent oversoul of Nature, whereas Jonathan Edwards believes in a world ruled by a sovereign God.
d. Ralph Waldo Emerson believes that individual consciousness will be lost after death, whereas Jonathan Edwards believes that the soul will go to heaven or hell.

463. Which of the following terms best defines the doctrine of Divine Election as discussed in the passage?

a. God's power
b. the soul's redemption
c. eternal damnation
d. predestined salvation

464. In the context of the passage, which of the following words would best fit in the blank?

a. loving
b. just
c. horrible
d. imperious

SET 71 (Answers begin on page 176.)

Discussions about literature, especially complex literature, sometimes seem difficult at first. But again, use what you've learned. Read the passage more than once. Try outlining it. Ask yourself, What is the main idea? What are the details that back up the main idea?

The fictional world of Nobel Prize winner Toni Morrison's novel *Sula*—the African-American section of Medallion, Ohio, a community called "the Bottom"—is a place where people, and even natural things, are apt to go awry, to break from their prescribed boundaries, a place where bizarre and unnatural happenings and strange reversals of the ordinary are commonplace. The very naming of the setting of *Sula* is a turning-upside-down of the expected; the Bottom is located high up in the hills. The novel is furthermore filled with images of mutilation, both psychological and physical. A great part of the lives of the characters, therefore, is taken up with making sense of the world, setting boundaries and devising methods to control what is essentially uncontrollable. One of the major devices used by the people of the Bottom is the seemingly universal one of creating a ____________—in this case, the title character Sula—upon which to project both the evil they perceive outside themselves and the evil in their own hearts.

465. Based on the description of the setting of the novel *Sula*, which of the following adjectives would most likely describe the behavior of many of its residents?

a. furtive
b. suspicious
c. unkempt
d. eccentric

466. Which of the following words would best fit into the blank in the final sentence of the passage?

a. scapegoat
b. hero
c. leader
d. victim

Ever since human beings began their conscious sojourn on this planet, they have puzzled over the riddle of evil and debated its source. Two concepts have predominated in the debate. The first of these holds that evil is an active force, a force of darkness as substantial and powerful as that of light. In terms of the individual human being, this force might be seen as the "Shadow" side of the personality, the feared side that the individual may deny but that is still a real and integral part of her or him. The second of the two concepts holds that evil is essentially ________, the absence of good, that darkness is not a thing in itself but rather the absence of light. In terms of the individual human being, this doctrine says that evil arises from a lack, a deprivation, from what John A. Sanford calls "a mutilation of the soul."

467. Which of the following phrases would best fit into the blank in the third sentence of the passage?
- a. perplexing
- b. passive
- c. capricious
- d. ephemeral

468. The main point of the passage is that
- a. human beings have long pondered the enigma of evil
- b. evil may be viewed as either a natural force or a human characteristic
- c. there are two long-debated, contradictory views of evil
- d. human beings are not likely ever to solve the problem of evil

469. Which of the following does an individual sometimes use to deal with the "Shadow" side of his or her personality?
- a. scorn
- b. love
- c. acceptance
- d. denial

SET 72 (Answers begin on page 177.)

Don't forget to look for the author's attitude in the material you read. Is it positive or negative or neutral? Ask yourself, How might the author have spoken if he or she had felt differently?

The English language premiere of Samuel Beckett's play *Waiting for Godot* took place in London in August 1955. *Godot* is an avant-garde play with only five characters (not including Mr. Godot, who never arrives) and a minimal setting: one rock and one bare tree. The play has two acts; the second act repeats what little action occurs in the first with few changes: the tree, for instance, acquires one leaf. In a statement that was to become famous, the critic Vivian Mercer has described *Godot* as "a play in which nothing happens twice." Opening night, critics and playgoers greeted the play with bafflement and derision. The line, "Nothing happens, nobody comes, nobody goes. It's awful," was met by a loud rejoinder of "Hear! Hear!" from an audience member. ______________________________. However, Harold Hobson's review in *The Sunday Times* managed to recognize the play for what history has proven it to be, a revolutionary moment in theater.

470. Judging from the information provided in the paragraph, which of the following statements is accurate?
a. The 1955 production of *Waiting for Godot* was the play's first performance.
b. *Waiting for Godot* was written by Peter Hall.
c. The sets and characters in *Waiting for Godot* were typical of London stage productions in the 1950s.
d. *Waiting for Godot* was not first performed in English.

471. Which sentence, if inserted in the blank space above, would make the best sense in the context of the passage?
a. The director, Peter Hall, had to beg the theater management not to close the play immediately but to wait for the Sunday reviews.
b. Despite the audience reaction, the cast and director believed in the play.
c. It looked as if *Waiting for Godot* was beginning a long run as the most controversial play of London's 1955 season.
d. *Waiting for Godot* was in danger of closing the first week of its run and of becoming nothing more than a footnote in the annals of the English stage.

472. Which of the following provides the best definition of the term "avant-garde" as the author intends it in the passage?
a. innovative
b. unintelligible
c. foreign
d. high-brow

473. Which of the following best describes the attitude of the author of the passage toward the play *Waiting for Godot*?
a. It was a curiosity in theater history.
b. It is the most important play of the 20th century.
c. It is too repetitious.
d. It represents a turning point in stage history.

SET 73 (Answers begin on page 177.)

When confronted with ideas that are unfamiliar, first boil the passage down to its main idea and supporting details. Again, an outline is an excellent way to simplify complex material and get at its meaning.

In his famous study of myth, *The Hero with a Thousand Faces*, Joseph Campbell writes about the archetypal hero who has ventured outside the boundaries of the village and, after many trials and adventures, has returned with the boon that will save or enlighten his fellows. Like Carl Jung, Campbell believes that the story of the hero is part of the collective unconscious of all humankind. He likens the returning hero to the sacred or tabooed personage described by James Frazier in *The Golden Bough*. Such an individual must, in many instances of myth, be insulated from the rest of society, "not merely for his own sake but for the sake of others; for since the virtue of holiness is, so to say, a powerful explosive which the smallest touch can detonate, it is necessary in the interest of the general safety to keep it within narrow bounds."

There is __________ between the archetypal hero who has journeyed into the wilderness and the poet who has journeyed into the realm of imagination. Both places are dangerous and full of wonders, and both, at their deepest levels, are journeys that take place in the kingdom of the unconscious mind, a place that, in Campbell's words, "goes down into unsuspected Aladdin caves. There not only jewels but dangerous jinn abide. . . ."

474. Based on the passage, which of the following would best describe the hero's journey?

a. wonderful
b. terrifying
c. awesome
d. whimsical

475. The title of Campbell's book, *The Hero with a Thousand Faces*, is meant to convey

a. the many villagers whose lives are changed by the story the hero has to tell
b. the fact that the hero journeys into many different imaginary countries
c. the many languages into which the myth of the hero has been translated
d. the universality of the myth of the hero who journeys into the wilderness

476. Based on the passage, which of the following best describes the story that will likely be told by Campbell's returning hero and Frazier's sacred or tabooed personage?

a. a radically mind-altering story
b. a story that will terrify people to no good end
c. a warning of catastrophe to come
d. a story based on a dangerous lie

477. Which of the following is the most accurate definition of boon as the word is used in the passage?

a. gift
b. blessing
c. charm
d. prize

478. The phrase that would most accurately fit into the blank in the first sentence of the second paragraph is

a. much similarity
b. a wide gulf
c. long-standing conflict
d. an abiding devotion

479. As depicted in the last sentence of the passage, "Aladdin's caves" are most likely to be found in

a. holy books
b. fairy tales
c. the fantasies of the hero
d. the unconscious mind

SET 74 (Answers begin on page 178.)

These next passages are light, informational pieces. What choices did the author make, in terms of tone and style, that cause them to seem less serious than some of other passages you've read?

The sentences are numbered in the first passage to help you answer the questions.

1) The Woodstock Music and Art Fair—better known to its participants and to history simply as "Woodstock"—should have been a colossal failure. 2) Just a month prior to its August 15, 1969, opening, the fair's organizers were informed by the council of Wallkill, New York, that permission to hold the festival was withdrawn. 3) Amazingly, not only was a new site found, but word got out to the public of the fair's new location.

4) At the new site, fences that were supposed to facilitate ticket collection never materialized, and all attempts at gathering tickets were abandoned. 5) Crowd estimates of 30,000 kept rising; by the end of the three days, some estimated the crowd at 500,000. 6) And then, on opening night, it began to rain. 7) Off and on, throughout all three days, huge summer storms rolled over the gathering. 8) In spite of these problems, most people think of Woodstock not only as a fond memory but as the defining moment for an entire generation.

480. Which of the following would be the most appropriate title for this passage?

a. Backstage at Woodstock
b. Woodstock: From The Band to The Who
c. Remembering Woodstock
d. Woodstock: The Untold Story

481. Which of the following numbered sentences of the passage best represents an opinion rather than a fact?

a. sentence 1
b. sentence 2
c. sentence 3
d. sentence 4

482. Why is the word "amazingly" used in sentence 3?

a. because the time in which the move was made and word sent out was so short
b. because the fair drew such an unexpectedly enormous crowd
c. because there was such pressure by New York officials against holding the fair
d. because the stormy weather was so unfavorable

O'Connell Street is the main thoroughfare of Dublin City. Although it is not a particularly long street, Dubliners will tell the visitor proudly that it is the widest street in all of Europe. This claim usually meets with protests, especially from French tourists, claiming the Champs Elysees of Paris as Europe's widest street. But the witty Dubliner will not relinquish bragging rights easily and will trump the French visitor with a fine distinction: the Champs Elysees is a *boulevard;* O'Connell is a *street.*

Divided by several important monuments running the length of its center, the street is named for Daniel O'Connell, an Irish patriot. ______________________________________. O'Connell stands high above the unhurried crowds of shoppers, business people, and students on a sturdy column, surrounded by four serene angels seated at each corner of the monument's base. Further up the street is the famous General Post Office that the locals affectionately call "the GPO." During the 1916 rebellion, the GPO was taken over and occupied by the Irish rebels to British rule, sparking weeks of armed combat in the city's center. To this day, the angels of O'Connell's monument bear the marks of the fighting: one sits reading calmly, apparently unaware of the bullet hole dimpling her upper arm; another, reaching out to stroke the ears of a huge bronze Irish wolfhound, has survived what should be a mortal wound to her heart.

483. Which of the following would be the best title for this passage?
- a. Dublin's Famous Monuments
- b. The Irish Take Pride in Their Capitol City
- c. The Widest Street in Europe
- d. Sights and History on Dublin's O'Connell Street

484. Which sentence, if inserted in the blank space above, would be the most correct and contribute the most pertinent information to that paragraph?
- a. His monument stands at the lower end of the road, that is, the end closest to the river Liffey that bisects Dublin.
- b. Other monuments along the street include statues to Charles Parnell, Anna Livia Plurabelle, and James Joyce.
- c. Dublin tourist buses leave from this site every twenty minutes.
- d. Daniel O'Connell was an important Irish nationalist, who died before the 1916 rebellion.

485. What is the best definition for the word underlined word trump as it is used in the first paragraph of the passage?
- a. to trumpet loudly, to blare or drown out
- b. to trample
- c. to get the better of by using a key or hidden resource
- d. to devise a fraud, to employ trickery

486. With which of the following statements about the people of Dublin would the author of the passage most likely agree?
- a. They are proud of their history but lack industry.
- b. They are playful and tricky.
- c. They are rebellious and do not like tourists.
- d. They are witty and relaxed.

SET 75 (Answers begin on page 178.)

Here is a pair of passages that have the same subject but entirely different purposes. As you read, think about tone and style. Compare the two approaches. Try to pick out individual words that further each writer's intent and support each writer's opinion. Look at each passage in terms of how it might have been written differently.

Excerpt from Chamber of Commerce brochure

Dilly's Deli provides a dining experience like no other! A rustic atmosphere, along with delicious food, provide an opportunity to soak up the local flavor. Recently relocated to the old market area, Dilly's is especially popular for lunch. At the counter, you can place your order for one of Dilly's three daily lunch specials or one of several sandwiches, all at reasonable prices. Once you get your food, choose a seat at one of the four charming communal tables. By the time you are ready to carry your paper plate to the trash bin, you have experienced some of the best food and most charming company our city has to offer.

Restaurant review

Yesterday I was exposed to what has been called "a dining experience like no other." At lunch-time, Dilly's Deli is so crowded that I wondered when the fire marshal had last visited the establishment. The line snaked out the door to the corner, and by the time I reached the counter, I was freezing. I decided on the hamburger steak special, the other specials being liver and onions and tuna casserole. Each special is offered with two side dishes, but there was no potato salad left and the green beans were cooked nearly beyond recognition. I chose the gelatin of the day and what turned out to be the blandest coleslaw I have ever eaten.

At Dilly's you sit at one of the four long tables. The couple sitting across from me was having an argument. The truck driver sitting next to me told me more than I wanted to know about highway taxes. After I had tasted each of the dishes on my plate, I rose to leave, whereupon one of the people working behind the counter yelled at me to clean up after myself. Throwing away that plate of food was the most enjoyable part of dining at Dilly's.

487. If you go to lunch at Dilly's Deli, you could expect to see
- a. a long line of customers
- b. the fire marshal
- c. the restaurant critic from the newspaper
- d. homemade pie

488. Both passages suggest that if you eat lunch at Dilly's Deli, you should expect to
- a. sit next to a truck driver
- b. place your order with the waiter who comes to your table
- c. dress warmly
- d. carry your own food to your table

489. Which of the following illustrates the restaurant critic's opinion of the food at Dilly's Deli?
- a. "At Dilly's you sit at one of the four long tables."
- b. "At lunch-time, Dilly's is so crowded, I wondered when the fire marshal had last visited the establishment."
- c. "After I had tasted each of the dishes on my plate, I rose to leave, whereupon one of the people working behind the counter yelled at me to clean up after myself."
- d. "Throwing away that plate of food was the most enjoyable part of dining at Dilly's."

490. The main purpose of the restaurant review is to

a. tell people they probably don't want to eat at Dilly's Deli
b. make fun of couples who argue in public
c. recommend the hamburger steak special
d. warn people that Dilly's Deli tends to be crowded

491. The main purpose of the Chamber of Commerce brochure is to

a. profile the owner of Dilly's Deli
b. describe in detail the food served at Dilly's Deli
c. encourage people to eat at Dilly's Deli
d. explain the historical significance of the Dilly's Deli Building

SET 76 (Answers begin on page 179.)

This set contains a fairly light, simple, and straightforward passage, yet the author's purpose is serious. Ask yourself what techniques the author uses to persuade. Which word choices reveal the author's attitude?

Greyhound racing is the sixth most popular spectator sport in the United States. Over the last decade a growing number of racers have been adopted to live out their retirement as household pets, once their racing career is over.

Many people hesitate to adopt a retired racing greyhound because they think only very old dogs are available. Actually, even champion racers only work until they are about three-and-a-half years old. Since greyhounds usually live to be 12–15 years old, their retirement is much longer than their racing careers.

People worry that a greyhound will be more nervous and active than other breeds and will need a large space to run. These are false impressions. Greyhounds have naturally sweet, mild dispositions, and while they love to run, they are sprinters rather than distance runners and are sufficiently exercised with a few laps around a fenced-in backyard everyday.

Greyhounds do not make good watchdogs, but they are very good with children, get along well with other dogs (and usually cats as well), and are very affectionate and loyal. They are intelligent, well-behaved dogs, usually housebroken in only a few days. A retired racing greyhound is a wonderful pet for almost anyone.

492. Based on the tone of the passage, the author's MAIN purpose is to
- a. teach prospective owners how to transform their racing greyhound into a good pet
- b. show how the greyhound's nature makes it equally good as racer and pet
- c. encourage people to adopt retired racing greyhounds
- d. objectively present the pros and cons of adopting a racing greyhound

493. According to the passage, adopting a greyhound is a good idea for people who
- a. do not have children
- b. live in apartments
- c. do not usually like dogs
- d. already have another dog or a cat

494. Which of the following is implied by the passage?
- a. The public is more aware of greyhounds than they used to be.
- b. Greyhounds are more competitive than other dogs.
- c. Greyhound racing should not be allowed.
- d. People who own pet rabbits should not adopt greyhounds.

495. One drawback of adopting a greyhound is that
- a. greyhounds are not good with children
- b. greyhounds are old when they retire from racing
- c. the greyhound's sensitivity makes it temperamental
- d. greyhounds are not good watch dogs

496. This passage is most like an advertisement because it
a. uses statistics to prove its point
b. does not present information to substantiate its claims
c. says nothing negative about greyhounds
d. encourages people to do something

497. According to the passage, a retired racing greyhound available for adoption will most likely be
a. happy to be retiring
b. easily housebroken
c. a champion, or else it would have been euthanized
d. less high-strung than those that are not available for adoption

SET 77 (Answers begin on page 179.)

This final set is a light piece. Read it for fun, but don't forget to ask yourself why the author wrote it just as she did. What word choices keep it from being technical and dry? How might she have written it in a different way for a different audience?

Cuttlefish are intriguing little animals. The cuttlefish resembles a rather large squid and is, like the octopus, a member of the order of cephalopods. Although they are not considered the most highly evolved of the cephalopods, they are extremely intelligent. While observing them, it is hard to tell who is doing the observing, you or the cuttlefish, especially since the eye of the cuttlefish is very similar in structure to the human eye. Cuttlefish are also highly mobile and fast creatures. They come equipped with a small jet located just below the tentacles that can expel water to help them move. Ribbons of flexible fin on each side of the body allow cuttlefish to hover, move, stop, and start. ____________ ____________________________________.

The cuttlefish is sometimes referred to as the "chameleon of the sea" because it can change its skin color and pattern instantaneously. Masters of camouflage, they can blend into any environment for protection, but they are also capable of the most imaginative displays of iridescent, brilliant color and intricate designs, which scientists believe they use to communicate with each other and for mating displays. However, judging from the riot of ornaments and hues cuttlefish produce, it is hard not to believe they paint themselves so beautifully just for the sheer joy of it. At the very least, cuttlefish conversation must be the most sparkling in all the sea.

498. Which of the following sentences, if inserted into the blank line, would best sum up the first paragraph and lead into the next.

a. The cuttlefish can be cooked and eaten like its less tender relatives, the squid and octopus, but must still be tenderized before cooking in order not to be exceedingly chewy.
b. On a scuba dive when you're observing cuttlefish, it is best to move slowly because cuttlefish have excellent eyesight and will probably see you first.
c. Cuttlefish do not have an exoskeleton; instead, their skin is covered with chromataphors.
d. By far their most intriguing characteristic is their ability to change their body color and pattern.

499. Which of the following is correct according to the information given in the passage?

a. Cuttlefish are a type of squid.
b. Cuttlefish use jet propulsion as one form of locomotion.
c. The cuttlefish does not have an exoskeleton.
d. Cuttlefish are the most intelligent cephalopods.

500. Which of the following best outlines the main topics addressed in the passage?

a. I. Explanation of why cuttlefish are intriguing
   II. Communication skills of cuttlefish

b. I. Classification and difficulties of observing cuttlefish
   II. Scientific explanation of modes of cuttlefish communication

c. I. Explanation of the cuttlefish's method of locomotion
   II. Description of color displays in mating behavior

d. I. General classification and characteristics of cuttlefish
   II. Uses and beauty of the cuttlefish's ability to change color

501. Which of the following best describes the purpose of the author in the passage?

a. to prove the intelligence of cuttlefish
b. to explain the communication habits of cuttlefish
c. to produce a fanciful description of the "chameleon of the sea"
d. to describe the "chameleon of the sea" informatively and entertainingly

ANSWERS

SET 1 (Page 6)

1. c. The first sentence speaks of rehabilitation as a way to *reduce crime.* The passage makes no mention of doing away with prisons (choice a). It does state that without rehabilitation, offenders will *usually* commit more crimes, but it does not say they *invariably* will (choice b). Choice **d** is not mentioned in the passage.
2. d. See the final sentence of the passage. The other choices may be true, but they are not in the passage.
3. d. The last sentence in the passage refers to dogs as probably the *oldest alarm system.* The other choices, even if true, are not in the passage.
4. a. See sentence two of the passage.
5. d. This is the only choice definitely reflected in the passage.
6. a. This is the only choice reflected in the passage. Choice **d** may seem attractive at first, but the passage simply says that the local media does not cover local politics—it doesn't give the reason for their neglect.
7. c. Sentence three indicates the importance of organization and design. The other choices, even if true, are not in the passage.
8. a. The first sentence reflects the idea that the Dvorak keyboard is more efficient than the QWERTY. The other choices are not in the passage.

9. **b.** The other choices are wrong because the passage is not concerned with how sanitation workers should deal with sharp objects, but with how everyone should dispose of sharp objects in order to avoid hurting sanitation workers.

10. **a.** See sentence two. The other choices are not reflected in the passage.

SET 2 (Page 9)

11. **d.** See the second sentence of the passage. The other choices are not in the passage.

12. **c.** See the final sentence of the passage. The other choices might be true but are not in the passage.

13. **a.** Sentence two speaks of *the greater productivity* of telecommuters. The other choices may seem attractive on the surface because they contain words and phrases from the passage, but a closer look will show them to be incorrect or absent from the passage.

14. **c.** The final sentence indicates that the atmosphere of Mars has been *stripped away.*

15. **c.** Note that the question does not ask for the main idea of the passage, only for an idea supported by the passage. Choice **b** may seem attractive at first, but a careful reading will show that the passage does not deal with unemployment.

16. **d.** The directions mention nothing about main or secondary roads.

17. **a.** The other choices may be true but are not mentioned in the directions.

18. **c.** The directions indicate that the City prefers, but does not require, use of the new container provided by the city, and that the customers may use more than one container if they purchase an additional one.

19. **b.** The directions state use of the new containers will *expedite pick-up of recyclables.* This indicates that the new containers will make the recycling program more efficient.

20. **b.** See the second and third sentences for the steps in making ratatouille. Only choice **b** reflects the correct order.

21. **d.** The main part of the passage describes how to cook vegetables. Only choice **d** indicates that vegetables are included in the dish. The other choices are not reflected in the passage.

SET 3 (Page 12)

22. **d.** The third sentence of the passage states that officers may refer to their notes. Choices **a** and **b** are not in the passage, and choice **c** is contradicted in the first sentence.

23. **a.** The passage states that officers should keep complete notes and use them to *refresh their memories* about events. None of the other choices is reflected in the passage.

24. **a.** This is stated in the first sentence of the passage. The other choices are not in the passage.

25. **d.** See the final sentence of the passage.

26. **c.** See the second sentence, which defines *ksa.* The other choices are refuted in the passage.

27. **d.** This answer is implied by the statement that redistribution is needed so that people in emerging nations can have proper medical care. Choices **a**, **b**, and **c** are not mentioned in the passage.

28. **c.** This choice is supported as the best answer because the paragraph indicates that legislators once feared suggesting gas taxes, but now many of them are pushing bills in favor of these taxes. There is no indication that choice **a** is true. Choice **b** is wrong because the paragraph doesn't say why more gas taxes are being proposed. There is no support for choice **d**.

29. **d.** This is the best answer because the paragraph directly states that warm weather affects consumers' inclination to spend. Choice **a** is wrong because even though there were high sales for a particular February, this does not mean that sales are not higher in other months. There is no support for **b.** Choice **c** presents a misleading figure of 4 million. The paragraph states that the record of 4.75 million was at an annual, not a monthly, rate.

SET 4 (Page 14)

30. **b.** This idea sums up the passage. Choice **a** is too narrow (the passage mentions fascism and democracy as well as communism and capitalism). Choices **c** and **d** are not in the passage.

31. **b.** Choices **a** and **c** are too narrow to be the main idea. Choice **d** simply supports the main idea, that lawyers have received undeserved criticism.

32. **c.** The third sentence is the main idea. It is a general idea that answers the only question posed in the passage. The other choices are not in the passage.

33. **d.** The passage states that the role of the *traditional* secretary is declining, not that secretaries are less important, so choice **a** is incorrect. Choices **b** and **c** are not in the passage.

34. **c.** This choice is closely related to all three sentences of the passage. Choice **a** is contradicted in the passage. Choices **b** and **d** are not in the passage.

35. **a.** The entire passage relates to this idea. The other ideas are not reflected in the passage.

36. **a.** This is the main idea of the passage because all the sentences relate to it. The other choices may be true but are not reflected in the passage.

37. **c.** This idea is expressed in the final sentence and wraps up the passage, speaking of the importance of *creating a balance.* The other choices are not in the passage.

38. **b.** The support for choice **b** is given in the second sentence of the paragraph. Generation Xers like to work independently, which means they are self-directed. No support is given for choice **a.** Choice **c** is not related to the paragraph. Although the paragraph mentions that Generation Xers liked to be challenged, it does not say they like to challenge their bosses' attitudes; therefore, choice **d** can be ruled out.

39. **d.** This choice encompasses the main information in the passage. Choices **a, b,** and **c** are not mentioned.

40. **a.** The title should express the main idea of the passage. The passage as a whole focuses on appropriate and inappropriate uses of e-mail. The other answer choices pick up more specific ideas that are expressed in the passage but are not its *main* idea.

SET 5 (Page 17)

41. **a.** The final sentence states that computer games and virtual reality help children *come to terms* with the truths of the real world. The other choices are not reflected in the passage.

42. **c.** The first and second sentences reflect this idea. The passage does not say that Native American art is dream-like (choice **a**). Choices **b** and **d** are too narrow to be main ideas.

43. **a.** This idea is expressed in two of the three sentences in the passage and sums up the overall meaning of the passage.

44. **d.** This is stated in the final paragraph. The other choices are not reflected in the passage.

45. **c.** This answer encompasses most of the information in the passage. Choice **a** is incorrect because the first sentence suggests that becoming hardened is unavoidable. Choices **b** and **d** are mentioned in the passage but are too narrow to be the main idea.

46. **b.** See the first two sentences of the passage.

47. **c.** The passage claims that becoming jaded is inevitable.

48. **b.** Choice **b** most nearly encompasses the whole passage. The other choices are too narrow to be main ideas.

49. **a.** The second sentence of the passage states that a PI may look into *insurance fraud scheme[s]* or a *philandering husband or wife.* The other choices may seem, at first glance, to relate to the passage but they are not actually in it.

SET 6 (Page 20)

50. **b.** This is the only choice reflected in the passage.

51. **a.** The passage is about confessions made to officers whom inmates believe to be fellow inmates. The passage does not say that inmates lose their privilege against self-incrimination (choice **b**), only that non-coerced confessions to undercover officers do not fall under that protection. The other two choices are not in the passage.

52. **d.** See sentence four of the passage.

53. **c.** This choice most nearly encompasses the passage and is reflected in the final sentence.

54. **b.** The passage defines an ecosystem as a community within which all members interrelate. (See the first three sentences of the paragraph.) Choice **a** is only one example of an interaction. The other two choices are also too narrow to sum up ecosystem activities.

55. **b.** This is the only choice that reflects the idea of interaction among all members of the group spoken of in the first sentence. The other choices are only physical settings.

SET 7 (Page 22)

56. **d.** The first two sentences of the passage indicate that a backdraft is dangerous because it is an explosion. The other choices are dangers, but they do not define a backdraft.

57. **b.** The second paragraph indicates that there is little or no visible flame with a potential backdraft. The other choices are listed at the end of the second paragraph as warning signs of a potential backdraft.

58. **c.** This is stated in the last paragraph. Choice **a** is not mentioned in the passage. The other choices would be useless or harmful.

59. **a.** The passage indicates that hot, smoldering fires have little or no visible flame and insufficient oxygen. It can reasonably be inferred, then, that more oxygen would produce more visible flames.

60. **c.** While choices **b** and **d** are also true, they are not the main idea; which is supported by the whole passage and spelled out in the last sentence. Choice **a** is wrong because not all suspects need to be read their Miranda rights, only those in custody.

61. **b.** This is implied in the next-to-last sentence.

62. **c.** See the first sentence of the passage.

63. **b.** The non-suspect must be informed of his or her freedom to leave the interrogation. Miranda rights are read only when the suspect is taken into custody, so choice **a** is incorrect. The right to an attorney (choice **c**) and the right to a phone call (choice **d**) are included in the Miranda rights.

SET 8 (Page 24)

64. **c.** The final sentence indicates that *people in working families* make up *51 percent* [of the poor] *under the current measure.* (The first sentence indicates that the current measure was introduced in 1963.)

65. b. The final sentence indicates that under the current measure, people in working families make up 51 percent of the poor; under the new measure they would make up 59 percent of the poor (this also refutes choice **a**). The proposed measure does not disregard expenses for basic needs (refuting choice **c**); it includes the value of non-cash benefits. The current measure identifies fewer people with health insurance (refuting choice **d**).

66. d. The discussion of carbon monoxide in the last paragraph serves to demonstrate why firefighters should wear breathing apparatus.

67. c. The dangers outlined in the first and second paragraphs of the passage are all caused by extreme heat.

68. b. The other choices are mentioned in the passage but are not the main idea.

69. a. The cooking temperature is given to show the difference of 1,000 degrees of heat between a motor vehicle fire and cooking.

70. b. The last paragraph states that *carbon monoxide... is odorless and colorless.*

SET 9 (Page 26)

71. b. See the first paragraph. Choice **a** is contradicted in the first paragraph. Choice **c** is perhaps true but is not in the passage. Choice **d** is incorrect because, although the president's assistant escorted Autherine Lucy to class, the passage does not say that the assistant *befriended* her—accompanying her to class may just have been his assigned job.

72. b. The first paragraph says that Autherine Lucy *bravely* took her seat, and the last paragraph refers to her *courage.*

73. a. According to the first paragraph, Autherine Lucy was surprised when the professor apparently did not notice her.

74. d. See the fourth sentence of the second paragraph.

75. c. The other answers are all contrary to information in the passage.

76. d. This is stated in the last paragraph (... *first aid measures should be directed at cooling the body quickly*). The other responses are first aid for heat exhaustion victims.

77. b. This is stated in the first sentence of the second paragraph. Choices **a** and **c** are symptoms of heat stroke. Choice **d** is not mentioned.

78. a. Heat stroke victims have a *blocked sweating mechanism*, as stated in the third paragraph.

79. b. This information is given in the second paragraph: If the victim still suffers from the symptoms listed in the first sentence of the paragraph, the victim needs more water and salt to help with the *inadequate intake of water and the loss of fluids* that caused those symptoms.

SET 10 (Page 28)

80. c. This title most nearly captures the main idea of the passage and the author's purpose in writing the piece. The other choices either are not mentioned or are secondary ideas in the passage.

81. b. This is the point of the second paragraph. It would be easy to get the wrong answer to this question by picking one you know to be true—for example, choice **a**—but which is not in the passage.

82. a. The first paragraph of the passage says that the food pyramid recommends six to eleven servings each day of grains and only two or three servings of meat.

83. d. See the second paragraph. The other choices are not mentioned in the passage.

84. c. This is implied in the first sentence of the passage.

85. d. This is the only choice that is important to the main point of the passage.

SET 11 (Page 29)

86. a. Sentence two states routine maintenance is performed by the maintenance department.

87. c. Sentence one states workers are responsible for refueling at the end of each shift; this implies taxicabs are refueled at the end of every shift.

88. d. The second sentence of the passage indicates that each driver who finishes a route will clean a truck.

89. a. The third sentence of the passage indicates that routes vary in the length of time they take to complete. The other choices are not included in the passage.

90. c. According to the last sentence of the passage, in the past city workers usually drove the same truck each day.

91. a. See the first sentence of the passage.

92. b. The third sentence tells what drivers should do *[i]f the bus is ahead of schedule.* The passage does not mention choice **a** or **c**, and the passengers' complaints have nothing to do how the bus "runs."

93. d. The whole passage deals with methods drivers should use to keep their buses from running ahead of schedule.

SET 12 (Page 31)

94. c. According to the passage, hazardous waste is defined by the United States Environmental Protection Agency.

95. d. The directions indicate that Harris should call the supervisor.

96. d. See paragraph one. (Paragraphs two and three make it clear that the Vehicle Maneuvering Training Buses are simulators.)

97. a. See the second sentence of paragraph two.

98. b. See the last sentence of the fourth paragraph.

99. c. Virtually the whole passage deals with F.A.S.T. membership requirements. The other choices are too narrow to be main ideas.

100. a. See the first paragraph.

SET 13 (Page 33)

101. c. Edith is trying to defraud the antique dealer by claiming that she owns an original by a famous poet. In option **a**, there is nothing to indicate that Bess altered any item or that she intended to defraud or harm anyone. She is not likely to expect anyone to believe that she is the Betsy Ross who created the first American flag. The same logic applies to option **b**. In **d**, Wendell has not tried to alter an object to increase its value, nor has he tried to defraud or harm anyone.

102. b. Rudy threatens to bash out the headlights on Edward's car, thereby threatening to damage another person's property. In the other options, there is no threat or apparent attempt to annoy, alarm, or torment anyone. The landlord in **d** is within his rights because the tenant is in arrears on her rent.

SET 14 (Page 34)

103. a. The passage says that thefts of electronic equipment take place on Mondays and Fridays between 4:00 p.m. and 8:00 p.m. This choice is the only one that covers those time spans.

104. b. According to the passage, car thefts take place on Moray Street between Elm and Chestnut on Saturdays and Wednesdays between midnight and 3:00 a.m.

105. c. See the second and final sentences of the passage.

SET 15 (Page 36)

106. d. The passage states that Mr. Pickens thought Mr. Morrow's companions *should be arrested.* Mr. Morrow himself is unconscious. Mr. Evans and Mr. Roland would probably be afraid of being blamed for Mr. Morrow's condition.

107. c. Mr. Morrow chugged a pint of whiskey in 15 minutes and is comatose.

108. a. The passage says that Mr. Morrow's friends' actions were *playful.*

109. a. According to Mr. Pickens, Mr. Morrow began to chug the whiskey at 12:10 and did so in about 15 minutes.

110. d. See the first sentence of the passage. The subway platform is where questioning occurred (choice **a**). The officers were initially in the uptown-bound train (choice **b**). The Fourth Street station was where the train was held until the officers arrived (choice **c**).

111. c. Although Miss Simpson allegedly assaulted the complainant and created a disturbance, she was arrested for the concealed weapon.

112. a. Alan Sterns is identified as the complainant in the second sentence of the passage.

113. d. See the next-to-last sentence.

114. a. According to Mr. Sterns, Miss Simpson struck him when he attempted to move her bags.

SET 16 (Page 38)

115. b. You can approach this question by asking *Why?* Mr. Hensley has forced open the door and has told police he is waiting for his wife. Choice **a** is incorrect; Mr. Hensley's child hid from him in a closet, and he evidently didn't try to get him to come out. Choice **c** is incorrect, because Mr. Hensley has a residence of his own at 1917 Roosevelt. Mr. Hensley evidently didn't intend peaceful reconciliation (choice **d**), since he kicked the door in.

116. d. You can approach this question by asking *Who?*. The first sentence of the passage states that the complaint was anonymous.

117. a. Asking *Why?* will help with this question. The officers drew their weapons because the door had been kicked in. They didn't know any of the other facts until they were inside the house.

118. c. Mr. Hensley spoke to the police *calmly*, and he made a seemingly matter-of-fact statement. There is no indication in the passage that Mr. Hensley was enraged at police or that he was remorseful or confused.

SET 17 (Page 39)

119. b. Raul Hernandez lives with his father at 122 Whitney Boulevard.

120. c. The last sentence says that Raul was charged with joyriding, not auto theft. His other violations are mentioned early in the paragraph: He first came to the officers' attention because he ran a stop light and was speeding; then they discovered he had no license.

121. c. The car's owner, Mr. Herrera, is the one who wants to charge Raul Hernandez.

122. a. The call came from William Gale.

123. d. The prowler was in the back yard at 213 Winston Street.

124. c. The last sentence makes it clear that Mr. Macy's offense was violating an Order of Protection.

SET 18 (Page 41)

125. d. Sentence four comes close to confirming choice **d.** The yelling the officers hear coming from inside Mr. Hayes' house is most likely Mr. Hayes, given all the circumstances described in the passage. The other choices are less certain as they are statements made by Mr. Weber when he was upset, and no witnesses are present to confirm them.

126. c. Alan Weber most likely made the call from his home at 1807 Clarkson.

127. a. According to the second sentence of the passage, Alan Weber told police he was *kept awake* by the noise coming from Mr. Hayes' home.

128. b. According to the passage, Mr. Hayes' first words to the police were *"It's about time you got here."*

129. a. According to the next-to-last sentence of the passage, Mr. Hayes told police he had *been protecting himself.*

130. c. The second sentence implies that Mr. Larkin, the victim, reported the crime.

131. d. The passage gives Ms. Fork's address as 210 Hawkins Drive, Apartment 3112.

132. a. The third sentence from the end states that Mr. Larkin, the victim, is the one who could not produce receipts for the stolen merchandise.

133. d. Clearly Mr. Cole, the suspect, may have stolen merchandise. However, since the serial numbers have been filed off the CD player and there is no way of knowing when this occurred, it is possible that it was stolen property when both Ms. Franklin, the neighbor, and Mr. Larkin, the victim, were in possession of it. The officers cannot know whether Ms. Franklin did indeed have possession of the merchandise and where it came from without further investigation.

134. d. The burglary took place while Mr. Larkin was at work from 10:00 p.m. to 8:15 a.m.

SET 19 (Page 43)

135. c. Although Steps 3 through 6 follow a reverse hierarchical order (from death to property damage), overall the instructions are presented in chronological order, beginning with logging on to the computer and ending with faxing copies of the forms to headquarters.

136. c. There was an injury, so form 103 must be completed, as stated in step 4 of the procedure. There was equipment damage, so form 107 must be completed, as stated in step 5 of the procedure. Step 8 says that form 106 must be completed for all fire reports. Step 7 says that form 122 must be completed, because forms 107 and 103 were both required

137. d. Since there was a death on the scene, form 111 must be completed, according to step 3 of the procedure. There was an injury, so form 103 must be completed, as stated in step 4 of the procedure. As always, form 106 must be completed, as stated in step 8 of the procedure.

138. a. Since there were no injuries, deaths, or equipment loss or damage, step 8 indicates that only form 106 must be completed.

SET 20 (Page 44)

139. a. The instructions are in hierarchical order, from most preferred to least preferred.

140. c. Interior stairs is the preferred method of removal.

141. c. The last item in the order of removal is the life net.

142. a. The fire escape immediately follows the adjoining building in the order.

143. b. Roof rescue rope follows the ladder as a means of egress.

144. d. The best choice is chronological order. Clues are given especially in Steps 2 and 3 (checking the air cylinder, then turning it on) and 6 and 7 (testing the unit, then shutting it down). Choice a is wrong because no one step is said to be more important than another. All steps are crucial, and the apparatus can be put out of service if it malfunctions at any step along the way.

145. c. See the paragraph that comes just before the list of procedures.

146. b. See Step 2 of the procedure.

147. c. The cylinder is turned on after completion of Step 2, which is checking the cylinder gauge.

SET 21 (Page 46)

148. b. The Guidelines are in chronological order, starting with finding a location for the roadblock through setting it up and proceeding on through arresting drunk drivers and other lawbreakers.

149. a. See Step 1 of the Guidelines.

150. d. See the final sentences of Step 6 of the Guidelines.

151. c. Step 5 of the Guidelines states that roadblocks should be limited to two hours; otherwise, they *will lose their effectiveness as word spreads... and motorists who have been drinking will avoid the area.* Choice **b** is incorrect because one-quarter of a mile is a short distance from the original roadblock location, and drunk drivers will likely avoid that area, too.

152. b. Step 3 of the Guidelines states that all cars must be stopped.

153. d. See Step 2 of the Guidelines.

154. a. See the fourth sentence of Step 4 of the Guidelines.

155. c. See Step 3 of the Guidelines.

156. a. See the introductory paragraph of the Guidelines.

157. b. See Step 5 of the Guidelines.

158. d. See the final sentence of Step 2 of the Guidelines.

SET 22 (Page 49)

159. b. See the list for compartment 2.

160. c. The ax is in compartment 1, the fire extinguisher in compartment 3.

161. d. The pry bar is in compartment 1, the tool box is in compartment 2, and the first aid kit is in compartment 4.

162. d. Kinds of damage are the topics covered by this list. There is no indication that the inspection must be done in any order, nor is one type of damage said to be more serious than another; all types are reasons to place the rope out of service.

163. b. The reasons for removing the rope from service does not specify age of the rope.

164. c. As per item 1 of the list, the rope was subject to the weight of two people.

165. c. The stain was removed and therefore is not *persistent*, so the rope can be returned to service.

SET 23 (Page 51)

166. d. A wind speed of 173 miles per hour falls between 158 and 206, which is the range for an F3 tornado, choice **d**.

167. b. Applying words such as *mild, moderate, significant, severe, devastating, cataclysmic,* and *overwhelming* to the damage done by a tornado is a means of describing the damage, therefore the words are *descriptive*, choice **b**.

SET 24 (Page 52)

168. b. 1,200 acres at Bramley Acres Resort and 526 acres at Stone River Park adds up to 1,726 acres.

169. c. The Voorhees fire occurred June 7. The Cougar Run fire occurred June 14.

170. c. The woman's actions constituted murder by way of arson (see June 25 on the table). Choices **a** and **d** would be accidents; choice **b** would be an act of nature.

SET 25 (Page 53)

171. c. Braxton, with 23 days, is at level three. (Note: According to research, lack of precipitation or abundance of precipitation does not necessarily equate with greatest fire potential.)

172. a. Livingston Center is at level three; Riderville is at level two.

173. a. The question asks in what field the most men are *involved,* not *employed.* The answer would include students, who are not necessarily salaried workers. Therefore, combining the number of students and teachers gives the largest number involved in education.

174. b. Only two of the 200 men in the Baidya caste are farmers.

SET 26 (Page 54)

175. c. The passage is mainly about types of behavior that would *cause* a legitimate Terry Stop.

176. b. See the first three sentences of paragraph one.

177. d. See paragraph four.

178. c. Based on the actions described, an officer's training and experience would indicate the people might be planning a robbery.

179. b. See paragraph one, sentence six.

180. a. See paragraph two.

181. c. See paragraph four.

182. d. See paragraph three, which states in part that sometimes it is wise to wait to arrest the suspect until a crime is in progress, *when patrol cars can be dispatched to arrest the individual.* In the scenario described in the passage, it appears that a crime is about to be committed at or after 5:00—it is now 4:30.

183. a. See paragraph one, sentences three and four.

184. b. See paragraph two, sentence four. Choice **a** might appear attractive at first, but the passage doesn't say shoplifters should *never* be frisked.

185. c. See paragraph two, sentence six.

SET 27 (Page 57)

186. a. Although cause-and-effect is involved in the second paragraph, the passage mainly follows a hierarchical order, beginning with evacuating the premises and ending with sharing information with the emergency personnel.

187. b. This choice gets broadest coverage in the passage. All other choices are mentioned, but are too narrow to be called the most important priority.

188. d. Choice **a** can be found in the last paragraph. Choice **b** can be found in the second paragraph. Choice **c** is mentioned in last sentence.

189. a. See last sentence, third paragraph.

190. c. Note that the word *because* appears in the first three paragraphs. The final paragraph does not literally use the word, but does speak of the reasons detectors should not be placed near windows (because of drafts) or in kitchen and garages (because of fumes).

191. b. Although the passage mentions firefighters' responsibilities (choice **a**), the main focus of the passage is the installation of smoke detectors. Choice **c** is only a detail. Choice **d** is not mentioned.

192. b. The answer can be found in the first sentence of the third paragraph. Choice **a** may seem attractive because the passage contains the words "four inches" and "twelve inches" but close reading will show it to be incorrect.

193. a. The answer is found in the first paragraph (*smoke detectors cut a person's risk of dying in a fire in half*).

194. c. The answer can be found in the next to last sentence of the passage.

195. d. The answer is implied by the first sentence of the passage. There is no information in the passage to indicate that the other choices are a firefighter's responsibility, even though they may be in certain real-life situations.

196. b. The second paragraph states that there should be a smoke detector *outside each sleeping area* in a home. The last sentence states that smoke detectors should NOT be placed in kitchens (choice **d**).

SET 28 (Page 60)

197. d. This passage is arranged mainly in chronological order (note the words *upon arriving*; *the occupants shall then*; and statements that signal moving on to the next step); however, cause-and-effect figures in, as well; the passage explains the reasons for the various steps in the procedure. Neither hierarchical order nor comparison-contrast are used to any great extent.

198. c. See the third paragraph.

199. a. This can be surmised based on next to last sentence.

200. d. See the third paragraph.

201. c. Choice **a** is mentioned in the fourth paragraph (*a check must be made near all gas appliances* implies that they are potential sources of contamination). Choice **b** is mentioned in the third paragraph (*CO poisoning symptoms* are listed). Choice **d** is mentioned in the second paragraph (calibrated meters should be taken onto the premises).

SET 29 (Page 61)

202. a. Although cause and effect are mentioned, and the passage speaks of the most important job of the firefighter, the passage is actually arranged in chronological order. Looking for potential causes comes first, then flagging evidence, then sharing the information that has been gathered.

203. c. See the next to last sentence.

204. a. See the fifth paragraph.

205. b. The fifth paragraph gives the steps to take after the fire is brought under control, and removal of evidence is not one of them.

206. a. The first sentence states that while fighting a fire, firefighters can take steps to *maximize efforts of investigators*. Virtually all of the passage deals with those steps. Do not confuse the "main idea" of the passage with the firefighter's "main responsibility" (option **b**). Options **c** and **d** are only details relating to the main idea.

207. b. The second paragraph states that personnel shall be kept away from flagged evidence, *unless doing so would hamper fire fighting efforts.*

208. d. This is a listing of reasons why the Charlesburg wildfire was so devastating.

209. c. See the second bulleted section. Choices **a** and **b** deal with residents, not fire companies. Regarding choice **d**, water sources were clearly located, although overall water supply posed a problem.

210. d. See the last sentence of the first bulleted section. All the other choices are fair assumptions but are not included in passage.

211. a. See the first sentence of the last bulleted section.

212. d. Choice **a** appears in the fourth bulleted section. Choice **b** appears in introduction. Choice **c** appears in last bulleted section.

SET 30 (Page 64)

213. a. Although written in paragraph form, this is really a list of instructions for the job of firefighter, arranged in chronological order, although causes and effects are discussed also. (Note the key words, *First, Next,* and *Finally.*)

214. a. Roughly in the middle, the passage states, *Review evacuation plans to make sure primary and secondary exits are viable.*

215. d. Near the end, the passage recommends replacing water-filled extinguishers with foam units, *which are safer.*

216. c. Choice **a** is mentioned in the sections on alarms. Choice **b** is mentioned in the third sentence. Choice **d** is mentioned near the conclusion. Blocked exits are mentioned near the middle of the passage, but there is no discussion of relevant procedures with regard to them.

217. d. Near the end, the passage advises replacing pressurized extinguishers if they are located near electrical equipment. The other options are not covered.

218. d. Only choice **d** is an explicit statement (hidden fires cause discoloration, etc.), although cause-and-effect may be inferred from the other statements.

219. b. The answer is found in the first sentence of the passage. The other choices give information from the passage, but they do not indicate the main purpose of an overhaul.

220. d. The answer is implied in the third sentence of the first paragraph in combination with the conditions described in the second paragraph.

221. b. The answer can be found in the last sentence. Choices **a, c,** and **d** are not in the passage.

SET 31 (Page 66)

222. b. Choice **b** includes the main points of the selection and is not too broad. Choice **a** features minor points from the selection. Choice **c** also features minor points, with the addition of *History of the National Park system,* which is not included in the selection. Choice **d** lists points that are not discussed in the selection.

223. d. Choice **d** expresses the main idea of paragraph four of the selection. The information in choices **a, b,** and **c** is not expressed in paragraph four.

224. a. Choice **a** is correct, according to paragraph two, sentence two. Choices **b** and **c** are mentioned in the selection, but not as causing the islands; choice **d** is not mentioned in the selection.

225. c. Paragraph five discusses the visitors to Acadia National Park, therefore, choice **c** is correct. Choices **a, b,** and **d** are not mentioned in the selection.

226. a. Sentence one, paragraph three states that the length of the Maine coastline is 2500 miles. Paragraph one states that the straight-line distance between Kittery and Eastport—not the length of the coastline—is 225 miles, so **c** is incorrect. Choices **b** and **d** are also incorrect.

SET 32 (Page 68)

227. c. Choice **c** provides the best outline of the passage. The other choices all contain points that are not covered by the passage.

228. b. This passage provides information to social workers about music therapy, as the title in choice **b** indicates. Choice **d** is incorrect because the first sentence speaks of mental and physical health professionals *referring* their clients and patients to music therapists; the second sentence indicates that *It* (meaning a *referral*) *seems a particularly good choice for the social worker.* Choice **c** is possible, but does not summarize the passage as well as choice **b**. Choice **a** refers to a topic not covered in the passage.

229. **d.** Although the other choices may be correct, they require knowledge beyond the passage. Based on the information in the passage, **d** is the best choice.

230. **a.** Based particularly on the last sentence of the passage, **a** is the best choice. The other choices are beyond the scope of the passage.

SET 33 (Page 70)

231. **c.** Throughout, the passage contrasts social conditions in 1868 with conditions in 1954 when the opinion was written.

232. **c.** Choice **c** provides the most complete and accurate organization of the material in this selection. The other choices contain information which is addressed only briefly, or not at all, in the selection.

233. **b.** This question tests the ability to define a word from context. More such questions follow shortly after this one. The passage discusses the negative effect of segregated schools on public school students, which indicates that the *plaintiffs* in the case were public school students. There is nothing in the selection to indicate that the plaintiffs were either without attorneys or public school teachers. The case is called *Brown v. Board of Education*; however, in the context of paragraph five, it is clear that the plaintiffs are the winners of the case and that public school students, not board members, prevailed in the case.

234. **d.** Throughout the passage there is discussion of the 14th Amendment and its date is given as 1868. This would indicate that the phrase "post-War amendments" refers to the 14th and other amendments passed after the Civil War, choice **d**. The other answer choices refer also to Constitutional Amendments, but the context indicates that these are not the amendments being discussed in the selection.

235. **a.** This question tests the ability to draw valid conclusions from details in a selection. the word reargument indicates that the arguments were made at least once before, therefore, choice **a** is correct. The other answer choices contain information that is not addressed in the selection and are therefore too specific to be accurate.

236. **b.** This question tests the ability to recognize the details that support a writer's argument. Paragraph 3 deals extensively with the state of public education at the time the 14th Amendment was passed, therefore, answer **b** is correct. The information contained in choices **a** and **c** is not indicated by the selection; nor does it appear that the Court simply disagreed with Congress, as stated in choice **d**.

SET 34 (Page 72)

237. **c.** To be *outmoded* is to be out-of-date or *obsolete.* The Kennel Club's computer system may also be worthless, unusuable, and even, in its current condition, unnecessary. However, the key to the meaning is the context—that is, the phrase *having been installed fifteen years ago.*

238. **c.** Something that is *menial* is subservient or *lowly*. The key to the meaning here is the phrase *as to be beneath him.*

239. a. To be *vindictive* is to be revengeful or *spiteful.* The keys here are the word *malice* and the phrase *almost ruined her career.*

240. d. When something is done *obstinately,* it is done in a refractory manner or *stubbornly.* The key here are the words *headstrong man.*

241. b. A *glib* remark is a quick and insincere, or *superficial,* one. The key here is the word *trivialized.*

242. a. A *panacea* is an all-encompassing remedy or *cure.* The key here is the phrase *answer to every problem.*

243. b. Something that is *nondescript* is without distinction or *undistinguished.* The keys here are the words *usually a flashy dresser* and *uncharacteristically.*

244. b. To be *ostentatious* is to be showy or *pretentious.* Choices **c** and **d** may be true, as well, but the key to the most likely meaning is the fact that the councilman has an *expensive, showy* car.

245. a. A *prerequisite* is something that is necessary or *required.* The fact that you can't join the team without the volleyball course means that it is required. The other choices do not imply a hard and fast rule.

246. c. To be held *accountable* is to be held answerable or *responsible.*

SET 35 (Page 74)

247. d. Something that is *animated* is vigorous or *lively.*

248. a. To be *diplomatic* is to be or sensitive in dealing with others or *tactful.*

249. b. When one is *compliant,* one is acquiescent or *obedient.*

250. c. To *augment* something is to add to or *expand* it.

251. b. When something is *intermittent,* it is *periodic* or starts and stops at intervals.

252. d. To be *inundated* is to be overwhelmed or *flooded.*

253. c. To be *unique* is to be one of a kind or *unparalleled.*

254. d. When one is incredulous, one is skeptical or *disbelieving.*

255. d. When one is *proficient* at something, one is expert or *skilled* at it.

256. a. When something is *tentative* it is of an *experimental* or *provisional* nature.

SET 36 (Page 76)

257. b. When a group's opinion is *unanimous* it is in accord or *uniform.*

258. a. To *alleviate* something is to make it more bearable or *ease* it.

259. c. To be *indispensable* is to be necessary or *essential.*

260. a. To *expedite* a process is to hurry it up or *accelerate* it.

261. b. If something is plausible, it is believable or *credible.*

262. c. To *infer* something is to *surmise* it or deduce it from the evidence.

263. d. An *ultimatum* is a final statement of terms or *non-negotiable demand.*

264. b. To be meticulous is to be extremely careful or *painstaking.*

265. b. To be *apathetic* is to show little or no interest or to be *indifferent.*

266. a. To be *fortified* is to be strengthened or *reinforced.*

SET 37 (Page 77)

267. d. To *delegate* a task is to *assign* it or to appoint another to do it.

268. c. To *arouse* someone is to stir up or *provoke* that person.

269. d. To *articulate* something is to give words to it or *express* it.

270. c. If something is *expansive*, it is broad, open, or *spacious*.

271. b. If a thing is *detrimental*, it is injurious or *harmful*.

272. b. *Crooning* and *warbling* both mean singing.

273. d. *Fallout* is a "side effect" that occurs as a result of some incident, action, or happening—that is, it's a consequence of something. It is the most logical word to describe something that affects a victim for years.

274. b. *Humid* and *damp* both mean the same thing in this context.

275. b. *Sphere* and *globe* both mean ball or orb.

SET 38 (Page 78)

276. d. To *decontaminate* and to *purify* both mean to remove impurities.

277. c. To be *tailored* and to be *altered* both mean to be made to fit.

278. a. *Dormant* and *inactive* both mean not active, as if asleep (the root meaning of *dormant*).

279. c. To be *banished* and to be *exiled* both mean to be forced to leave.

280. b. *Yielded* and *relinquished* both mean given up.

281. c. A *journal* and a *diary* are both records of daily happenings.

282. b. To be *jostled* is to be *bumped*.

283. a. A *hostel* and an *inn* are both lodging places for travelers.

284. a. *Philosophy* means a system of motivating *principles*.

SET 39 (Page 79)

285. a. To *consider* is to think about. The other choices make no sense in context.

286. c. An *opportunity* is a chance. The other choices make no sense.

287. b. The key here is the phrase, *We knew nothing about Betty....* The word is in the context of something hidden or secret. The other choices are not related to being in the dark about a person.

288. b. A *grimace* is a contortion of the face. Neither a *wrinkle* nor a *simper* match the descriptive word *ferocious*. A *shriek* would be described in terms of how it sounds, rather than how it looks.

289. d. Answers **a** and **c** do not include the sense of hierarchy conveyed in the phrase *to enforce social order*. Answer **b** does convey a sense of hierarchy but in the wrong order.

290. a. This is the choice that makes most sense when combined with the word *rocky*.

291. b. Although a muscle that atrophies may be *weakened* (choice c), the primary meaning of the phrase *to atrophy* is *to waste away*.

SET 40 (Page 80)

292. a. The passage implies that having a manager who was eccentric and entertaining would be a good thing. That is, the context of the word is positive, so a positive, or at least neutral, word would most likely correct. Except for **a**, the choices are all negative.

293. a. To depict the Sami, the author uses words that point to their gentleness, which is an admirable quality: They move *quietly*, display *courtesy* to the spirits of the wilderness, and were known as *peaceful retreaters*. There is nothing pitying, contemptuous, or patronizing in the language, and nothing in the passage indicates that the author is perplexed—the description of the Sami is clear and to the point.

294. b. The immediate context of the word *animistic* defines the word: *for [the Sami], nature and natural objects had a conscious life, a spirit.* There is no indication in the passage that the author believes the Sami's animistic religion is *irrational* (choice **a**). The other choices are not in the passage.

295. c. Throughout the passage the author displays a positive attitude toward the Sami and their beliefs. Although they are said to be *peaceful*, they are not said to be timid or fearful (they retreated from war because *they did not believe* in it). In the context of the passage, it's most likely that the Sami *avoid making a disturbance* in the wilderness out of *respect* for the spirits.

SET 41 (Page 81)

296. b. This choice mentions *factors* to be weighed, leading directly into the next sentence about age, weight, and general health.

297. d. The mention that searching for spices have *changed the course of history* and that, for spices, *nations have… gone to war* implies that the subject of the paragraph is history. These phrases also connote danger and intrigue.

298. c. The mention of all the amazing things the brain is capable of is directly relevant to its being *mysterious and complex.* The other choices are less relevant.

SET 42 (Page 82)

299. a. This choice refers both to age and complexity; **b** and **c** refer only to complexity. Answer **d** is less relevant to the topic sentence (which doesn't mention Darwin or theories) than the other choices.

300. d. None of the other choices would lead to anything like *fascination*; they're just dry facts.

301. c. The topic sentence speaks of the Big Bang theory's being much misunderstood, and **c** addresses this, whereas the other choices do not.

SET 43 (Page 83)

302. b. *Susceptible* means being *liable to be affected by something.* According to the sixth paragraph, some patients are genetically predisposed, or susceptible, to some diseases.

303. a. The next-to-last sentence of the second paragraph indicates that the report *advised caution in using… predictive tests.*

304. b. See the last sentence of the sixth paragraph, which states that *effective treatment can be started in a few hundred infants.*

305. d. The first paragraph says that the report addressed concerns about *protecting confidentiality.*

306. c. The last sentence of the fourth paragraph states that *careful pilot studies… need to be done first.*

307. d. See the fifth paragraph: *Newborn screening is the most common type of genetic screening today.*

SET 44 (Page 85)

308. d. The second sentence of the first paragraph states that probes record responses. The second paragraph says that electrodes *accumulate much data.*

309. c. The tone throughout the passage suggests the potential for microprobes. They can be permanently implanted, they have advantages over electrodes, they are promising candidates for neural prostheses, they will have great accuracy, and they are flexible.

310. d. According to the third paragraph, people who *lack* biochemicals could receive doses via prostheses. However, there is no suggestion that removing biochemicals would be viable.

311. a. The first sentence of the third paragraph says that microprobes have channels that *open the way for delivery of drugs.* Studying the brain (choice d) is not the initial function of channels, though it is one of the uses of the probes themselves.

SET 45 (Page 86)

312. b. Throughout, the passage compares and contrasts the various methods of medical waste disposal.

313. d. See the last sentence of the third paragraph. Compaction may well reduce transportation costs (choice **a**) according to the third paragraph. That it reduces the volume of waste (choice **b**) is an advantage, not a disadvantage. Compaction is not designed to eliminate organic matter, so confirming that it has been eliminated (choice **c**) is not an issue.

314. a. See the last sentence of the fifth paragraph, which states that *incineration is... the preferred method for on-site treatment.*

315. b. See the last sentence of the sixth paragraph, which points out that steam sterilization does not change the appearance of the waste, thus perhaps raising questions at a landfill.

316. c. The fourth paragraph states that liquid is separated from pulp in the hydropulping process. The sixth paragraph says that liquid may form during the sterilization process.

317. a. This response relies on an understanding of pathological wastes, which are wastes generated by infectious materials. The seventh paragraph points out that incineration is especially appropriate for pathological wastes. Previously, the sixth paragraph had said that steam sterilization is appropriate for substances contaminated with infectious organisms.

318. d. The second paragraph says that the main risk of pushing carts is potential exposure from torn bags but that automated carts can reduce that potential.

319. b. See the next-to-last last sentence of the fourth paragraph. Sterilization does not change the appearance of waste. While compacting does change the volume of the waste, it is not appropriate for eliminating hazardous materials.

320. d. See the second sentence of the second paragraph: *there is some risk of exhausting contaminants into hallways,* meaning waste might be discharged.

321. b. See the last sentence of the passage, which states, regarding the rotary kiln, that *the costs have been prohibitive for smaller units.*

322. c. Although the contaminants may sometimes be extremely toxic (choice **a**), the word *fugitive* here is the key to the meaning. The words *fugitive emissions* are used in the context of the disposal process of hydropulping, and to be a fugitive means to run away or to escape, so the logical choice, given this context, is choice **c**. There is nothing anywhere in the passage about criminal activity, so choice **b** isn't a likely answer. Choice **d** is wrong because the *microbiological testing* the passage speaks of pertains to making sure all waste is disposed of.

SET 46 (Page 89)

323. b. Spina bifida aperta is the more severe form of spina bifida in which a noticeable sac protrudes from the infant's back. No post-surgical mortality rates are given in this passage.

324. d. Hyperactivity was not mentioned in the passage as a possible result of spina bifida.

325. c. In the second paragraph, the author states that the higher a myelocele is on the spinal column, the more severe the disability. The cervical vertebrae are the highest vertebrae listed in the question and answer choices.

326. c. Hydrocephalus is the correct term and is given in the final paragraph of the passage.

327. a. The first four sentences of paragraph two discuss this topic. Meningoceles are small sacs that produce no muscular paralysis once repaired. A myelocele, also known as a meningomyelocele, refers to an actual portion of the undeveloped spinal cord that protrudes from the spine.

328. d. The passage concludes with the thought that although spina bifida is a serious condition, sufferers may lead productive lives. The other options are either never stated or are false.

329. c. Paragraph one says that in spina bifida the bones of the spinal column *do not close properly*, so choice **c** is the most logical. None of the other choices are related to lack of closure.

SET 47 (Page 91)

330. a. Choice **b** emphasizes only damage to the atmosphere; the passage encompasses more than that. Choice **c** does not mention the atmosphere, which is the main focus of the passage. Choice **d** is too narrow—the final paragraph of the passage emphasizes that the circulation of the atmosphere is but one example of the complex events that keeps the earth alive.

331. c. This question assesses the ability to see the organization of a reading passage and to organize material for study purposes. Choice **a** is wrong because the passage does not explain exactly what will happen as a result of damage to the atmosphere and other life-sustaining mechanisms. Choice **b** is wrong because the passage does not explain the origin of the atmosphere. Choice **d** is wrong because it is solar energy that travels 93 million miles through space, not the atmosphere.

332. b. The *biosphere*, as defined in the first paragraph, is a *region* (or part) of the earth; it is not the envelope around the earth, the living things on earth, or the circulation of the atmosphere (choices **a**, **c**, and **d**).

333. d. This question assesses the ability to recognize supported and unsupported claims. Choice **a** deals with solar radiation, not with circulation of the atmosphere. Choice **b** is an assertion without specific supporting detail. Choice **c** describes how the atmosphere protects earth but does not speak of the circulation of the atmosphere. Only choice **d** explains that conditions would be unlivable at the equator and poles without the circulation of the atmosphere; therefore, it is the best choice.

334. a. This question assesses the ability to see cause-and-effect. The second paragraph deals with how variations in the strength with which solar radiation strikes the earth affects temperature. None of the other choices is discussed in terms of all temperature changes on earth.

335. a. There is no mention in the first paragraph of any *reviving* or *cleansing* effect the atmosphere may have (choices **b** and **d**). In a sense, enabling the earth to sustain life is *invigorating*; however, choice **a** is a better choice because the first two sentences talk about how the atmosphere *protects* the earth from harmful forces.

SET 48 (Page 94)

336. d. The first paragraph mentions that the symptoms of Type-II diabetes may occur gradually and thus be attributed to other causes. Left untreated, diabetes can cause damage to several major organs in the body.

337. b. According to the beginning of the second paragraph, only the long-term health problems are the same for these two different disorders.

338. d. Paragraph two mentions that when the body has more glucose than needed, it stores the overflow in muscle tissue, fat, or the liver.

339. c. According to the last paragraph, non-insulin dependent diabetics should stick to a diet consisting of 50–60 percent carbohydrates. The paragraph also notes that raw foods do not cause as high a blood sugar level as cooked foods.

340. a. The fourth paragraph mentions that, although insulin must bind to a receptor in order to begin working, the main role of insulin is to signal the burning of glucose/sugar for energy. Most hormones function as stimuli for other processes.

341. b. Type II, or non-insulin-dependent, diabetes is the main subject of the passage, which distinguishes Type II from Type I and goes on to stress the importance of diet.

342. d. The fourth paragraph of the passage tells us that possible problems with insulin receptors include a paucity of receptors or a defect causing improper binding of the insulin to the receptors. In addition, even though insulin may bind to its receptors, cells may fail to read the signal to metabolize the glucose.

343. c. The second paragraph states that normally, after the digestive system breaks down food into smaller molecules, including glucose (otherwise known as sugar), the blood sugar level rises. Insulin is then released from the pancreas, thus signaling tissues to metabolized the glucose.

344. c. Type I diabetes is the insulin-dependent form of this condition. The minority of diabetics are afflicted with this form. They are diagnosed as children and must take daily injections of insulin to make up for what their pancreases do not produce.

345. a. The final paragraph says that there is no cure for diabetes, so choices **b** and **d** are incorrect). Choice **c** is a possibility, but consider the sound of the word *soothe.* It does not fit with the objective tone of the passage nearly as well as the word *counteract.*

SET 49 (Page 97)

346. d. Many asthma sufferers have an inherited tendency to have allergies, referred to as *atopy* in the third paragraph.

347. b. The fourth sentence of the second paragraph explains that during an attack the person afflicted with asthma will compensate for constricted airways by breathing a greater volume of air.

348. c. The first sentence of the passage begins, *No longer,* indicating that in the past asthma was considered an anomalous inflammation of the bronchi. Now asthma is considered a chronic condition of the lungs.

349. b. An exacerbation is usually defined as an aggravation of symptoms or increase in the severity of a disease. However, in this passage, *exacerbations* is interchangeable with *asthma attacks.*

350. a. Although cramping may occur during asthma attacks, it is not mentioned in the passage. See the bottom half of the second paragraph for a full explanation of the morphological effects of an attack.

351. d. The third paragraph discusses triggers in detail. While using a fan in the summer months sounds good, an air conditioner is recommended when the pollen count is high. Family pets and cigarette smoke are all distinctly inflammatory to asthma sufferers. Only physical activity is touted as a possible symptom reducer.

352. a. Since asthma symptoms vary throughout the day, relying on the presence of an attack or even just on the presence of a respiratory ailment to diagnose asthma is flawed logic.

353. b. All of the individuals listed would glean a certain amount of knowledge from the passage; however, a health care professional would find the broad overview of the effects of asthma, combined with the trigger-avoidance and diagnosis information, most relevant. A research scientist would likely know all of this information already. A mother with an asthmatic child would probably not be interested in the diagnosis protocol. The anti-smoking activist probably would not find enough fodder in this article.

354. d. According to the last part of the third paragraph, second-hand smoke can increase the risk of allergic sensitization in children.

SET 50 (Page 100)

355. c. In the first paragraph, the communication network of the millions of cells in the immune system is compared to bees swarming around a hive.

356. b. All of the answers indicate peaceful coexistence. However, according to the fifth sentence of the second paragraph, in this instance the state is referred to as self-tolerance.

357. c. See the last paragraph. The antigens known as allergens are responsible for triggering an inappropriate immune response to ragweed pollen.

358. d. The last paragraph of the passage mentions that an antigen *announces its foreignness* with intricate shapes called *epitopes* that protrude from the surface.

359. a. Every individual's immune system must learn to recognize and deal with nonself molecules through experience. However, the last section of the second paragraph mentions that the immune system is capable of choices **b**, **c**, and **d**.

360. b. According to the second paragraph, the ability to distinguish between self and nonself is the heart of the immune system. This topic is set up in the first paragraph and further elucidated throughout the body of the passage.

361. b. The last paragraph mentions that tissues or cells from another individual may act as antigens EXCEPT in the case of identical twins whose cells carry identical self-markers.

362. a. The context leads to the meaning: The first sentence speaks of complexity, from which we can infer an elaborate system of interconnections, especially in light of the second sentence. There is no mention of confusion in the passage (choice **b**). The word *perplexity* means bewilderment and is unrelated to the passage (choice **c**). Choice **d** is a newspaper and TV term that is unrelated to the passage.

SET 51 (Page 102)

363. b. See paragraph two, which states: *To deliver the gene into the TIL, the scientists used a virus, exploiting its natural tendency to invade cells.*

364. d. See paragraph three. The enzyme ADA is missing from patients with severe combined immunodeficiency disease.

365. a. The possibility of a cancer vaccine is discussed at the end of the passage. Included in the vaccine procedure is taking bits of tumor from a patient, treating those pieces of tumor with immune-cell-activating cytokines, and reinjecting the patient with the cancerous (albeit genetically altered) growths. The tobacco plant does not play a role in this vaccine, and the safety of gene transfer was proven in 1989, according to the passage.

366. c. The first paragraph says that yeast, bacteria, and mammalian cells in culture have been used to create human proteins. Viruses (choice **d**) are used to deliver the genetic material to target cells in other organisms.

367. d. According to the third paragraph, ADA is delivered to the T cells by a modified retrovirus.

368. b. Look closely at the immediate context of the word being defined. The sentence following the underlined term begins *Also called genetic engineering, recombinant DNA technology….* This means the two terms are synonymous or mean the same thing. (Choice **a** is one possible outcome of recombinant DNA technology but is not a synonym.) Choice **c** is a step in the process but is not the process. SCID is a disease and thus is the wrong choice.

SET 52 (Page 104)

369. b. See the third paragraph: *one in ten* (10 percent of) cases of anorexia end in death.

370. a. See the second and third paragraphs for reference to heart problems with anorexia, the fourth and fifth paragraphs for discussion of heart problems with bulimia, and the last paragraph where heart disease is mentioned as a risk in obese people who suffer from binge-eating disorder.

371. c. Near the end of the last paragraph, the passage indicates that binge-eating disorder patients experience *high* blood pressure.

372. d. It is the other way around—fifty percent of people with anorexia develop bulimia, as stated near the end of the fifth paragraph.

373. b. The first sentence of the fifth paragraph tells us that bulimia sufferers are often able to keep their problem a secret, partly because they maintain a normal or above normal weight.

374. c. In the second paragraph, the thyroid gland function is mentioned as slowing down—one effort on the part of the body to protect itself.

375. a. According to the second paragraph, dehydration contributes to constipation.

376. b. As stated in the opening sentence of the fourth paragraph, bulimia patients may exercise obsessively.

377. d. See the second sentence of the sixth paragraph. If as many as one-third of the binge-eating disorder population are men, it stands to reason that up to two-thirds are younger women, given that we have learned that about 90 percent of all eating disorder sufferers are adolescent and young adult women.

SET 53 (Page 107)

378. a. See the second sentence of the passage.

379. c. See the first sentence.

380. d. This reason is implied throughout the passage.

381. **a.** Since the subject of the passage is Internal Affairs—the department that investigates misconduct—the word *cronyism* most logically relates to police cover-up of wrongdoing, something that Internal Affairs is charged with preventing.

382. **c.** The passage presents two reasons for punishment. The second sentence notes a view that "some people" hold. The first line of the second paragraph indicates "another view."

383. **b.** This is the main idea of the first paragraph.

384. **a.** This is an application of the main idea of the second paragraph to a specific crime.

385. **d.** The second paragraph notes that one reason behind the deterrence theory is the effect of deterring not only criminals but also the public.

386. **a.** The last sentence of each paragraph specifies the effect of the theory discussed on the amount of discretion allowed to judges in sentencing.

SET 54 (Page 109)

387. **c.** See paragraphs 3 and 4. The other answer choices are mentioned in the passage but are too narrow to be the main idea.

388. **b.** See the last sentences of paragraph one, which discusses the stalking victim's *worst fear.*

389. **d.** All of the other choices are mentioned in the third paragraph. The victim's knowledge or lack of knowledge about anti-stalking laws is not discussed in the passage.

390. **a.** As discussed in the first paragraph, a restraining order is a civil remedy that is often not taken seriously by the stalker. Choice **b** seems close, until you realize that the third paragraph speaks of *some* stalkers, not *most.*

391. **a.** See paragraph two.

392. **c.** All of the other choices are mentioned or implied in the final paragraph.

SET 55 (Page 111)

393. **a.** The discussion of the traits of a person with anti-social personality disorder in the middle of the passage specifies that such a person does not have distortions of thought; therefore, the person would not have *delusions* of any kind. The passage speaks of the anti-social person as being "inordinately self-confident" (choice **b**) and of the person's *emotional shallowness* (choices **c** and **d**).

394. **d.** The third sentence of the passage speaks of *con games.* None of the other professions would suit an impulsive, shallow person who has been in trouble with the law.

395. **b.** The passage mentions *emotional shallowness.* The other choices hint at the capability to feel meaningful emotion.

396. **b.** The passage says that a person with anti-social personality disorder can mimic real emotion, thereby conning prison officials, judges, and psychiatrists. The other choices are mentioned in the passage, but not in connection with getting out of trouble with the law.

SET 56 (Page 112)

397. **d.** In the northern hemisphere, June 21 would be summer; however, according to the passage, it is the beginning of winter in the southern hemisphere.

398. **b.** Logically, if June 21 is called the summer solstice in the northern hemisphere, then that same day would be the winter solstice in the southern hemisphere.

399. **d.** Because the author mentions that one of the two women gained international fame because she attended the international conference, the reader can surmise that for a woman to attend was a rare occurrence; therefore, choice **d** is the best answer. Choices **b** and **c** are beyond the scope of the passage. Choice **a** might be true, but would require information not contained in the passage.

400. d. See the final sentence of the passage.

401. d. Choice **d**, *cave-ins*, makes most sense in context. It is indicated by the detail *deep underground* and the mention of an *immediate* and *ever-present* threat. While choice **a**, *black lung*, is a concern of miners, it is not an immediate fear, since it is a disease acquired over time. Choices **b** and **c** are not hinted at in the passage.

SET 57 (Page 114)

402. d. Answer **d** is the most accurate conclusion because the first sentence speaks of *periods of war.* The other choices, whether true or false, are not addressed in the selection.

403. b. Since the first customer of a Pyramid scheme must be allowed to make money, it can be inferred that the con artist who sets up the scheme must have the patience to wait through the first success.

404. d. The entire passage is about the great variety of people who become skyjackers and the resulting unpredictability of the crime. The last sentence says that because of this unpredictability, it is difficult to create an accurate profile. Choice **a** is wrong because the passage says that the crime is unpredictable, not that each individual skyjacker is. Choice **b** is not in the passage. Choice **c** is wrong because the passage does not speak in either-or terms but rather in terms of a *range.*

SET 58 (Page 115)

405. d. Although the people in the other choices might read this passage, it is not directed toward scholars (choices **a** and **b**), nor is there anything in it about operating a loom (choice **c**). The light informative tone, and the subject matter of the final sentence particularly, indicate that the passage is directed toward interior decorators.

406. a. Choices **b** and **d**, may be true, but they are beyond the scope of the passage, and a reader could not tell if the author believed them. Choice **c** reflects a traditional view that the author probably does not hold; the passage indicates that the author approves of a change in this attitude.

407. a. The passage explicitly states that Charlemagne was crowned emperor in 800 and died in 814—a period of 14 years. Therefore, **b**, **c**, and **d** are mathematically incorrect.

408. b. Although all of the choices are possible definitions of *culture*, the passage is speaking of a community of inter-related individuals—Europeans.

409. b. The missing sentence is in a portion of the passage which is discussing the long-term impacts of the Franks, therefore, **b** is the best choice. Choices **a** and **c** are written in a style appropriate to the passage, but the information is not appropriate. Choice **d** is more informal in style than the rest of the passage.

SET 59 (Page 117)

410. b. Choice **b** best reflects the writing style of the passage, which is for a general audience. Choices **a** and **c** are too informal; choice **d** uses pretentious jargon, which the rest of the passage avoids.

411. a. Either **a** or **b** are possible definitions of speculation, however, the passage suggests that in this case the author is referring to a theory—choice **a**. The other choices are vaguely similar, but are not accurate, based on the passage as a whole.

412. d. This passage is written in a style directed to a general audience; therefore, choices **a** and **b** are not correct as they are aimed toward specialized audiences. Nor is this passage in the style of a personal essay (choice **c**), which would contain impressions and conclusions. The articles in general circulation magazines are aimed toward wide audiences, as is this passage.

413. **b.** The context of the passage indicates that the sentences in question are pointing out an unforeseen consequence (however) and the current situation (now). The other choices would result in meanings that do not fit with the flow of information in the rest of the passage.

414. **d.** Choices **a**, **b**, and **c** are not supported by information in the passage. Thus, the best choice is **d**.

415. **d.** Choices **a** and **c** are possible definitions of ushered, but do not fit in the context of the passage. Choice **b** is an incorrect definition. *Heralded*, choice **d**, is the best definition in the context.

SET 60 (Page 119)

416. **b.** This is an inference question. Because the writer indicates that visitors to Hershey's Chocolate World are greeted by a giant Reeses Peanut Butter Cup, it would be logical to assume that these are manufactured by Hershey. Although the writer mentions the popularity of chocolate internationally, you cannot assume that it is popular in every country (choice **a**), nor is there any indication that Milton Hershey was the first person to manufacture chocolate in the U.S. (choice **c**). Choice **d** is not discussed in the passage at all.

417. **d.** This question tests your ability to use context clues to determine the intended meaning of a word. In paragraph three, the passage says *The Hershey Chocolate company was born in 1894 as a subsidiary of the Lancaster Caramel Company.* This indicates that a subsidiary company is one controlled by another company, choice **d.** While it may be true that Milton Hershey owned each company in its entirety (choice **a**), that is not clear from the material. There is also not indication that the chocolate company was created to support the caramel company (choice **b**). Finally, the passage contains no discussion of whether any of Hershey's companies were incorporated (choice **c**).

418. **a.** Choice **a** is the best choice because it is the most complete statement of the material. Choices **c** and **d** focus on small details of the passage; choice **b** is not discussed in the passage.

419. **b.** Paragraph three states that Hershey sold the caramel company six years after the founding of the chocolate company. The chocolate company was founded in 1894; the correct choice is **b**.

420. **c.** The Chicago International Exposition was where Hershey saw a demonstration of German chocolate making techniques, which indicates, along with the word *international* in its title, that the exposition contained displays from a variety of countries, choice **c**. None of the other choices can be inferred from the information in the passage.

421. **b.** There is nothing inherently dramatic, undignified, or rewarding discussed in paragraph 1. *Modest* is the word that best fits being born in a small village and having the unremarkable early life described; it is also a word that provides a contrast to the mention of Milton's later *popularity*.

SET 61 (Page 121)

422. **b.** The blank is followed by a discussion of the shortcomings of the RDA approach. Choice **a** is incorrect because it does not lead into the discussion that follows regarding the RDA approach's shortcomings. Choice **c** is incorrect because it is contradicted by the final sentence of the passage, which states that the RDA approach remains a *useful guide.* Choice **d** is incorrect because its slangy style is inconsistent with the style used in the rest of the passage.

423. **b.** Choice **b** is indicated by the final sentence, which indicates that the RDA approach is useful, but has limitations, implying that a supplemental guide would be a good thing. Choice **a** is contradicted by the final sentence of the passage. Choice **c** is incorrect because the passage says the RDA approach is a *useful guide*, but does NOT say it is the best guide to good nutrition. Choice **d** is contradicted by the next-to-last sentence of the passage.

424. **b.** The passage contains objective information about accounting such as one might find in a textbook. There is nothing new or newsworthy in it (choice **a**). The passage does not contain the significant amount of personal opinion one would expect to find in an essay (choice **c**). It does not deal with matters that might involve government (choice **d**).

425. **d.** The final sentence emphasizes the importance of correct interpretation of financial accounting. Choice **a** is wrong, because something so important would not be discretionary (optional). Choice **b** may be true, but it is not as important for guidelines to be convenient as it is for them to rigorous. Choice **c** is wrong because the word *austere* connotes sternness. People may be stern, but inanimate entities, such as guidelines, cannot be.

426. **b.** Choices **a**, **c**, and **d** are all listed in the passage as functions of accounting. On the other hand, the second sentence of the passage speaks of a *marketing department*, separate from the *accounting department.*

SET 62 (Page 123)

427. **a.** The final sentence is an instance of a regular pattern that still has an uncanny quality. Choices **b** and **c** would introduce a sentence with an idea contradicting the preceding. Choice **d** would indicate that the final sentence is a restatement of the preceding, which it is not.

428. **d.** The passage says that people in general consider genius *supernatural, but also... eccentric*; the pairing of *extraordinary* and *erratic* in choice **d** includes both meanings given in the passage. Choices **a** and **c** cover only one side of the passage's meaning. Choice **b** contains definitions that the passage does not ascribe to the common view of genius.

429. **c.** This title covers the main point of the passage that, while there are predictable patterns in the life of a genius, the pattern increases the sense of something supernatural touching his or her life. Choices **a** and **b** are too general. Choice **d** is inaccurate because the passage does not talk about disorder in the life of a genius.

430. **c.** All the other statements are inaccurate.

SET 63 (Page 124)

431. **c.** Rites are mentioned in the passage but are not described (choice **a**). The passage states that *vodoun* is not a superstition (refuting choice **b**). The etymology of the word *vodoun* (choice **d**) is in the passage but is too narrow to be the main point.

432. b. The discussion of the *etymology* of the word *vodoun* comes immediately after the assertion that *The word vodoun is believed to have come from the West African country of Benin*—that is, right after a discussion of the origin of the word *vodoun*.

433. c. This is the only choice that is subject to a debate which cannot be settled by research into historical facts.

434. d. Mention in the passage that attempts have been made to outlaw some of the practices of *vodoun*, and that it has been regarded by some as superstition, points to prejudice. The passage refutes choice **a**; it implies that *vodoun* is not a monotheistic belief system by use in the last sentence of the words *However* and *although*. Choices **b** and **c** do not appear in the passage.

435. d. Although answers **a**, **b**, and **c** may all be true, only **d** is used by the author to directly compare *vodoun* with mainstream religion.

SET 64 (Page 126)

436. c. This choice best captures the main theme. All the other choices are mentioned in the passage but are minor points.

437. b. This is implied in the first paragraph.

438. a. We can infer that Rachel is traveling alone simply because no one else is mentioned. Any of the other choices could also be true, but there is nothing in the passage to support them.

439. d. This choice is the only one that is implied within the passage, which says that Rachel is "searching for excitement." The other choices could also be true, but we can't know for sure without further information.

440. b. See the first paragraph. The other choices also happen to be true of Carnival, but they are not mentioned in the passage.

441. d. The last line of the passage shows Rachel headed from her hotel room to the street where Carnival is taking place. Thus, a logical continuation is for Rachel to be experiencing the adventure she is "determined to find."

SET 65 (Page 128)

442. a. In paragraph 2, Sylvia is described as *restless* and in paragraph 4 she is fearful of the impending storm; therefore her mood is most likely anxious. Choice **b** is wrong because there are no details that would indicate anger. Choices **c** and **d** are refuted because of her obvious dread of the coming storm.

443. d. Choices **a** and **b** may be true but are not reflected in the story segment. Choice **c** is wrong because the birds that surround Sylvia at work are dead and mounted and therefore aren't singing. In the final sentence, Sylvia is described as *mildly claustrophobic*, so the best answer is **d**, which states that she works in a space that *feels open*.

444. b. In paragraph four, Sylvia does not want to go outside because an electrical storm is coming, and she has always been *terrified* of storms. Choice **a** is wrong because the adjective *gloomy* (choice **a**) doesn't connote the threat of a frightening electrical storm. Since Sylvia is afraid of the weather, such cheery adjectives as *spring-like* or *bracing* (choices **c** and **d**) cannot be said to describe it.

445. a. Sylvia's job suits her partly because her boss is usually gone and she's alone at work; she is mildly fearful of meeting the new person, Lola Parrish and even thinks of leaving before their appointment. These details point to a distant kind of person, the opposite of someone who might be overbearing or malicious (choices **b** and **d**). She seems to want to be alone and so is unlikely to be dependent on others (choice **c**).

446. a. Sylvia does seem distant and her life somewhat cold, so choice **a** is the most logical choice. The details in the story segment do not connote lightness or airiness (she's restless and fearful; the weather is threatening), so choice **b** isn't logical. There is no hint in the story segment that Sylvia feels anything about her boss, nor is there anything in this scene to remind us of the actual killing of the birds in the museum (choices **c** and **d**).

SET 66 (Page 130)

447. b. The eagle, who *watches from his mountain walls* and falls *like a thunderbolt*, is depicted as too alert and dynamic to be dying (choice **a**). There is really no joy depicted in the poem nor any sense that this is a baby eagle (choice **c**), and there is no mention of baby birds he might be watching over (choice **d**). Saying that the eagle *watches* and then falls *like a thunderbolt* implies alertness and striking, so the most logical choice is that the eagle is hunting.

448. b. The word *azure* means blue and is often used to describe the sky. Neither a forest nor cliffs are azure (choices **a** and **c**), and nature is not mentioned as an entity in the poem (choice **d**).

449. a. It is the *wrinkled sea* that *crawls* in the first line of the second stanza of the poem.

SET 67 (Page 131)

450. b. The *fellow* frightens the speaker. **a**, **c**, and **d** are not frightening.

451. a. *Tighter breathing* indicates fear, as does *zero at the bone* (one is sometimes said to be cold with fear). Also, the subject is a snake, which is generally feared animal.

452. c. In context, the speaker is discussing animals, because he follows with his contrasting attitude toward *this fellow*, meaning the snake. The other choices are all human beings.

453. b. Stanza three contains the phrase *when a boy* implying the speaker was a boy in the past and is now, therefore, an adult man. (This is the reason it cannot be the poet speaking, her name being "Emily.")

SET 68 (Page 132)

454. b. The poem describes nature in terms of the murder of a happy flower, and includes the words *beheads* and *assassin*; therefore, the most logical description of the poet's attitude would not be *delight*, *indifference*, *reverence*, or *indifference*, but rather *dismay*.

455. b. The frost *beheads* the flower, and therefore can be thought of as an *assassin*. None of the other choices in the poem directly commits murder.

456. c. The flower in the poem is *happy* and feels *no surprise* that it must die, which implies *acceptance*. If there is any hint of *fear* or *horror* in the poem (choices **a** and **b**) it is on the part of the poet. Nothing in the poem is described as feeling *reverence* (choice **d**).

457. c. A God who would *approve* of a *happy flower's* being beheaded, while apparently the rest of the natural world (as exemplified by the sun) remains *unmoved* is probably not to be regarded as *benevolent* or *just* (choices **a** and **b**). Approval does not connote *anger* (choice **d**). The most logical choice is that, in this poem, God is *cruel* (choice **c**).

SET 69 (Page 133)

458. **b.** The answer is **b**, because the connotations of words like *bonds* and *constraints* in the passage suggest a *confined space* of criticism where the mind must be allowed to find some movement or *play.* None of the other choices make sense.

459. **a.** According to the passage, Blake believed that, *through art* (that is, *through the reordering of sense impression by the creative imagination*) *true religion is revealed.* Artistic inspiration (choice **c**) might be involved, but the words *religion* and *moment of vision* point towards a mystical experience, rather than a primarily artistic one. There is no mention in the passage of *Christianity* (choice **b**) and no hint that the author views Blake's *moment of vision* as a false perception (*hallucinatory experience,* choice **d**).

460. **a.** The passage's tone and word choice (*true religion* and *eternity... revealed* through art) indicate that the world at *the moment of vision* is reality. There is no hint in the passage that nature represents a state of innocence for Blake (choice **b**)—the contrary is implied. The idea that nature is made up of *base and corrupt material* or that it will *perish* (choices **c** and **d**) are not in the passage.

SET 70 (Page 134)

461. **a.** The final sentence states that *Nature will not mind drowning a man or a woman,* and sentence 4 speaks of Edwards' approval of God's *arbitrary* will; neither Nature nor God, as described in the passage, would notice *the fall of a sparrow.* Choice **b** is incorrect because Edwards has a *delightful conviction* in *God's sovereignty* (authority or power), which indicates that he believes God's judgment, no matter how arbitrary, is wise. Choices **c** and **d** are incorrect because Emerson speaks of Nature's intention as *harmony and joy.*

462. **b.** This choice says *how* the reflections of Emerson and Edwards are alike (that is, their acceptance of the arbitrary nature of Nature and God) and also speaks of the irony of the similarity between Emerson and Edwards, which is mentioned in the passage. Choice **a** is true, but is too general, since it does not say exactly how the two philosophers are alike. Choice **c** and **d** are incorrect because they emphasize differences between the two world views, whereas the passage emphasizes similarities.

463. **d.** To be elected means to be chosen, and the passage speaks of *God's choosing according to his divine and arbitrary will, whom he would to eternal life* (i.e., to salvation). Being rejected is the opposite of being chosen or elected, so someone rejected would be damned (choice **c**). The other choices do not reflect an element of choice.

464. **c.** The word *horrible* most definitely contrasts to the words *exceedingly pleasant, bright, and sweet,* and the words *formerly* and *however* indicate that the sentence is describing a contrast. The other choices do not necessarily point to a contrast.

SET 71 (Page 136)

465. **d.** The passage says of the people who live in "the bottom" that they are *apt to go awry,* to *break from their natural boundaries.* A person who is *eccentric* is quirky or odd. Nowhere in the passage is it implied that the people are *furtive, suspicious,* or *unkempt* (choices **a**, **b**, and **c**).

466. **a.** A *scapegoat* is one who is forced to bear the blame for others or upon which the sins of a community are heaped. Choices **b** and **c** are wrong because nowhere in the passage is it implied that Sula is a hero or leader, or even that "the bottom" has such a personage. Sula may be a *victim* (choice **d**), but a community does not necessarily *project evil* onto a victim or an outcast the way they do onto a scapegoat, so choice **a** is still the best answer.

467. b. The first side of the debate says that evil is an *active force*; the opposing side would then see evil as just the opposite—something *passive*. Choice **a** is reflected in the first sentence. Human beings are *puzzled* (therefore perplexed) by evil but their puzzlement is not one of the two *concepts* of evil discussed in the passage. Choices **c** and **d** are not reflected in the passage at all.

468. c. The whole passage is a description of the debate between two concepts of evil. Choice **a** is mentioned in the passage but only by way of introduction to the description of the debate. Choices **b** and **d** are not in the passage.

469. d. The fourth sentence states that the "Shadow" side of the personality is something *the individual may deny*. The other choices are not in the passage.

SET 72 (Page 138)

470. d. The first line of the passage describes the *English language premiere* of the play, indicating it had previous performances in a different language.

471. d. It is logical that a play would close after such a bad first night reception, and the sentence in choice **d** also uses a metaphor about stage history that is extended in the next sentence. Choices **a**, **b**, and **c** do not fit the sense or syntax of the paragraph, since the *however* in the next sentence contradicts them.

472. a. While the other choices are sometimes connotations of the term *avant-garde*, the author's meaning of *innovative* is supported by the final judgment of the passage on the play as *revolutionary*.

473. d. Although the writer seems amused by the negative criticisms of the play, she does give the opinion that it was *revolutionary* (a word which literally means *a turning point*). Choice **a** underplays and choice **b** over-estimates the importance of the work to the author of the passage. Choice **c** is contradicted by the last sentence of the passage.

SET 73 (Page 139)

474. c. The word *awe* implies mingled reverence, dread, and wonder, so the adjective *awesome* is the best of all the choices to describe a place that is *dangerous and full of wonders* (second sentence of the second paragraph). Choices **a** and **b** both describe a part of the hero's journey but neither describes the whole of it. Choice **d** is incorrect because the hero's journey is described in the passage in very serious terms, not in *whimsical* (playful or fanciful) terms at all.

475. d. The first sentence of the passage describes Campbell's hero as *archetypal*. An archetype is a personage or pattern that occurs in literature and human thought often enough to be considered universal. Also, in the second sentence, the author of the passage mentions *the collective unconscious of all humankind*. The *faces* in the title belong to the *hero*, not to villagers, countries, or languages (choices **a**, **b**, and **c**).

476. a. The passage states that the hero's tale will *enlighten* his fellows, but that it will also be *dangerous*. Such a story would surely be radically mind-altering. Choice **b** is directly contradicted in the passage. If the hero's tale would terrify people *to no good end*, it could not possibly be enlightening. There is nothing in the passage to imply that the tale is a warning of catastrophe or a dangerous lie (choices **c** and **d**).

477. **b.** The definition of the word *boon* is *blessing.* What the hero brings back may be a kind of gift, charm, or prize (choices **a**, **c**, and **d**), but those words do not necessarily connote blessing or enlightenment.

478. **a.** The paragraph describes only the similarity between the hero's journey and the poet's. The other choices are not reflected in the passage.

479. **d.** The last sentence in the passage says that *the kingdom of the unconscious mind* goes down into *unsuspected Aladdin caves.* The story of *Aladdin* is a fairy tale (choice **b**), but neither this nor the other choices are in the passage.

SET 74 (Page 141)

480. **c.** The titles in choices **a**, **b**, and **d** all imply that the passage will provide information which it does not. Choice **c** is the most accurate choice because the passage deals mainly with remembering the fair.

481. **a.** Sentence 1 (choice **a**) contains the phrase *should have been a colossal failure,* which is an opinion of the author. The other choices are sentences that provide factual information about Woodstock.

482. **a.** The sentence preceding and leading into sentence 3 speaks of the very brief time—a month—that the organizers of the fair had to find a new site and get information out. Choices **b** and **d** are incorrect because they could not have been known about at the time the fair was moved. Choice **c** is incorrect because there is no indication in the passage that New York officials tried to stop the fair's moving or information getting out.

483. **d.** The title *Sights and History on Dublin's O'Connell Street* touches on all the specific subjects of the passage—the sights to see on this particular street and the history connected to them. Choice **a** is too general about the place described, which is a particular street in Dublin, not the whole city. Choices **b** and **c** are too specific in that they cover only the material in the first paragraph.

484. **a.** This choice sticks to the subject, Daniel O'Connell, announced in the sentence before it, and provides a transition to the sentence following it, a description of O'Connell's monument, by providing information about the location of the statue. Choices **b** and **c** swerve off topic, and choice **d** essentially repeats information given elsewhere in the paragraph.

485. **c.** The hidden or key resource mentioned in the passage is the fine distinction between the definition of *street* and *boulevard,* which is used to win the argument with or *get the better of* tourists. Choices **a** and **b** do not make sense; answer **d** is incorrect because there is no real fraud used in the argument in the passage.

486. **d.** The author offers an example of Dublin wit and mentions the *unhurried* pace of Dublin crowds. Choice **a** interprets the adjective *unhurried* in too pejorative a manner for the tone of the passage. Answers **b** and **c** similarly interpret the playful joke on French tourists too negatively.

SET 75 (Page 143)

487. **a.** This is implied in the first passage, which says that Dilly's is "popular," and the same idea is explicitly stated in the second passage.

488. **d.** This is the only one of the choices that is implied in both passages, which describe ordering at the counter.

489. d. This is the only quotation from the second passage that reveals the critic's opinion of the quality of the food.

490. a. The fact that the overall tone of the passage is quite negative points to the writer's purpose.

491. c. In contrast to the second passage, the first passage seems to be encouraging a visit to Dilly's. Answers **a** and **d** are not mentioned in the passage.

SET 76 (Page 145)

492. c. The tone of the passage is enthusiastic in its recommendation of the greyhound as pet and thereby encourages people to adopt one. It does not give advice on transforming a greyhound (choice **a**). Except to say that they love to run, the passage does not spend equal time on describing the greyhound as racer (choice **b**). The author's tone is not objective (choice **d**), but rather enthusiastic.

493. d. See the last paragraph. The passage does not mention **b** or **c**. Choice **a** is clearly wrong; the passage states the opposite.

494. a. See in the first paragraph. Choices **b**, **c**, and **d** are not touched on in the passage.

495. d. See the last paragraph. Choices **a**, **b** and **c** are contradicted in the passage.

496. d. The enthusiastic tone of the passage seems meant to encourage people to adopt retired greyhounds. Choice **a** is wrong because there is only one statistic in the passage (in the first sentence), and it is not used to prove the point that greyhounds make good pets. Choice **b** wrong because the author substantiates every point with information. Choice **c** is wrong because the passage does make the negative point that greyhounds do not make good watchdogs.

497. b. See the end of the next-to-last sentence in the passage. Choices **a**, **c**, and **d** are not to be found in the passage.

SET 77 (Page 147)

498. d. Choice **d** sums up the first paragraph, which is essentially a list of the cuttlefish's characteristics, by declaring which is the most interesting characteristic, and the sentence introduces the subject of the second paragraph—the ability of the cuttlefish to change color. Choice **a** adds information not in keeping with the tone or focus of the passage. Choice **b** repeats information in the first paragraph but does not introduce the next one. Choice **c** uses but does not explain scientific language, which is out of keeping with the general informational style of the passage.

499. b. The passage describes the cuttlefish's use of a water jet to move. Choice **a** is incorrect because the passage only describes cuttlefish as *resembling* squid. Choice **c** is a true characteristic, but is not mentioned in the passage. Choice **d** is incorrect because the passage never describes cuttlefish as the *most* intelligent cephalopod.

500. d. Choice **d** covers the most important ideas in the two paragraphs. All the other choices choose more minor details from the paragraphs as the main subjects.

501. d. Choice **d** includes both the informational content and light tone of the passage. Choices **a** and **b** describe too scientific an aim for the content and tone. Choice **c** does not include the informational content of the passage.

489. d. This is the only statement that the second [illegible] paragraph [illegible] of the quality of the [illegible].

490. a. The fact that the overall tone of the passage is quite negative points to the writer's [illegible].

491. c. In contrast to the second passage, the first passage seems to be [illegible] from [illegible] answers [illegible] not [illegible] in the passage.

SET 76 (Page [illegible])

492. c. The tone of the passage [illegible] its recommendation of the [illegible] that [illegible] encourage people [illegible]. It does not give advice on [illegible] and [illegible] about [illegible] to [illegible].

493. b. [illegible] the passage does not spend equal time on describing [illegible] Choice b [illegible] for [illegible].

494. d. [illegible] the passage [illegible] clearly wrong [illegible].

495. a. [illegible] choice b, c, and d [illegible] in the passage.

496. [illegible] paragraph [illegible] the passage.

497. [illegible] the passage [illegible] and d are not mentioned in the passage.

SET 77 (Page [illegible])

498. c. [illegible] character [illegible] the passage [illegible] the second [illegible] and is [illegible] of the passage [illegible] in the first paragraph [illegible] to the general [illegible] style of the passage.

499. b. [illegible] passage [illegible] choice [illegible] that [illegible] to the [illegible] to the passage. Choice d is incorrect because [illegible].

500. d. Choice [illegible] the most important idea in the two paragraphs [illegible] paragraphs as the [illegible].

501. d. Choice d includes both the informational [illegible] and [illegible] the [illegible] of the passage.

NOTES

[illegible] EXPRESS ADVANTAGE

[illegible] and Help You Succeed in School and in the Work[illegible]

[illegible]